CRYSTAL THERAPY

STEPHANIE HARRISON is principal of the International College of Crystal Healing (ICCH). She is a professional lecturer and vibrational healer and travels extensively both in the UK and overseas, training healers. Tim Harrison specializes in training healers to develop and strengthen their own energy fields. He is currently the chairman of the Affiliation of Crystal Healing Organizations (ACHO).

New Perspectives

THE SERIES

New Perspectives provide attractive and accessible introductions to a comprehensive range of mind, body and spirit topics. Beautifully designed and illustrated, these practical books are written by experts in each subject.

Titles in the series include:

ASTROLOGY
by Janis Huntley

BUDDHISM
by John Snelling

CHAKRAS
by Naomi Ozaniec

COLOUR THERAPY
by Pauline Wills

CRYSTAL THERAPY
by Stephanie & Tim Harrison

HERBAL REMEDIES
by Vicki Pitman

I CHING
by Stephen Karcher

NUTRITIONAL THERAPY
by Jeannette Ewin

RUNES
by Bernard King

SHAMANISM
by Nevill Drury

TAI CHI
by Paul Crompton

YOGA
by Howard Kent

New Perspectives

CRYSTAL THERAPY

An Introductory Guide to Crystals for Health and Well-Being

STEPHANIE AND TIM HARRISON

ELEMENT

Shaftesbury, Dorset • Boston, Massachusetts
Melbourne, Victoria

First published in Great Britain in 2000
by Element Books Limited, Shaftesbury, Dorset SP7 8BP

Published in the USA in 2000 by
Element Books, Inc.
160 North Washington Street,
Boston, MA 02114

Published in Australia in 2000 by Element Books
and distributed by Penguin Australia Limited,
487 Maroondah Highway, Ringwood,
Victoria 3134

Designed for Element Books Limited by
Design Revolution, Queens Park Villa,
30 West Drive, Brighton, East Sussex BN2 2GE

ELEMENT BOOKS LIMITED
Editorial Director: Sarah Sutton
Project Editor: Kelly Wakely
Commissioning Editor: Grace Cheetham
Production Director: Roger Lane

DESIGN REVOLUTION
Editorial Director: Ian Whitelaw
Art Director: Lindsey Johns
Project Editor: Nicola Hodgson
Editor: Julie Whitaker
Designer: Vanessa Good

Printed and bound in Great Britain by
Bemrose Security Printing, Derby

British Library Cataloguing in Publication
Data available

Library of Congress Cataloging in Publication
Data available

ISBN 1-86204-739-1

Contents

Acknowledgements

We would like to offer our gratitude to all the people who have helped with the writing of this book: in particular, Barbara Kleiner for her support and in-depth research; Andrew Wells BSc MSc FGA for verifying the geological and gemmological information; Lisa Carter for her help with background research and Grace Cheetham for her understanding and encouragement. We would also like to thank all the ICCH students and healers who helped us to formulate the guidelines and notes that formed the basis of this book. Special thanks to Georgina Chester who several years ago initiated the writing of this book.

Above all we would like to thank the Angelic Teachers, Guardians of the Light and Keepers of the Crystals who have lovingly supported us at all times.

To our darling daughter, Alicia,
and our dear parents.

The publishers wish to thank AKG London Picture Library for the use of the picture on page 28.

INTRODUCTION

This book is offered with love, from the heart. It is based on our truth, which has evolved over the years through our experiences as teachers and healers. It is our hope that it will serve to introduce you to the amazing world of crystals and inspire you to bring the crystalline frequency into your life.

We feel that all healing originates from one ultimate Divine source, which we variously refer to as Light, Great Spirit, Universal Love, Energy or God. Please substitute our words for the ones that best suit your personal philosophies and belief systems.

Our aim is to provide a spiritually-structured and supportive environment in which each individual can discover their own Divinely-guided way of working with crystals. We hope this book will help you to find your spiritual truth whilst exploring the fascinating crystal realm.

Wishing you love, light and joy.

Stephanie and Tim Harrison
Esher, Surrey, 1999

WHAT IS CRYSTAL THERAPY?

CHAPTER ONE

Crystal therapy is the use of crystals and gems to promote and restore a harmonious, balanced and therefore healthy state of being within the patient. It is a complementary therapy that works on all levels of the patient – physical, emotional, mental and spiritual.

Crystal therapy works on the principle that when the mind, body and spirit of a person are in balance and harmony, health will be the result. Imbalances can cause the body to become ill-at-ease or dis-eased, and this is when illness can occur.

As crystal therapy is a holistic treatment, most therapists work on the whole energy system of the patient, not just specific parts. Crystal therapy, like most forms of healing, helps to activate and promote the body's own self-healing mechanism.

Therefore, ultimately it is not the therapist, nor the crystals that do the healing, but the

LEFT CRYSTALS AND GEMSTONES ARE USED HOLISTICALLY TO HELP RESTORE EQUILIBRIUM OF MIND, BODY AND SPIRIT.

patients themselves – the crystals and the therapist merely support the self-healing process.

Until recently, crystals were considered to have specific healing properties. Crystal therapy, therefore, primarily consisted of matching the disease or symptoms with the appropriate crystal. However, more and more crystal therapists are discovering that crystals cannot be so simplistically categorized and that this approach actually limits the applications of crystals and

ABOVE ALLOW YOURSELF TO BE GUIDED BY INTUITION WHEN CHOOSING A CRYSTAL.

their healing possibilities. Two crystals of the same variety will not necessarily have identical healing properties. Moreover, different patients can receive very different healing experiences from the same crystal.

This more holistic and individual approach presents certain difficulties to the crystal therapist. We are frequently asked 'what is this crystal good for?' or 'what crystals will cure my headache, arthritis, etc?' Our response is 'which crystal(s) will serve your highest good and address the root cause of the problem or imbalance?' It is therefore extremely important that crystal therapists are able to choose the most appropriate crystals and the optimum method of application for a client.

However, it is frequently easier to choose crystals for yourself. Crystals are extremely effective self-healing tools, and there are simple yet powerful techniques that allow complete novices to harness the healing powers of crystals for themselves.

WHAT IS A CRYSTAL?

The strict gemmological definition of a crystal is a solid mineral substance with a regular internal atomic structure and an external form made up of flat faces arranged in a geometric shape. Examples of commonly found natural crystal formations are cubes of the mineral pyrite, octahedra of fluorite and six-sided prisms of quartz. Given ideal growing conditions, such as the right temperature and sufficient space, crystals are able to form naturally into an array of spectacular and intricate yet precise geometric shapes.

LEFT CRYSTALS ARE ENTIRELY NATURAL IN THEIR FORMATION, ALTHOUGH THEIR BEAUTY SOMETIMES MAKES THIS HARD TO BELIEVE.

Those unfamiliar with crystals often find it hard to believe that the incredible beauty and amazing symmetry of crystals is completely natural. They insist that crystals must be human creations, which have been artificially carved into these geometric shapes and their surfaces machine-polished. The fact is that crystals are completely natural works of art created by Mother Earth.

Many 'crystals' that are used by crystal therapists have a perfect internal atomic structure that gives the possibility of a crystal being formed. However, the external form may not always be a perfectly shaped crystal with flat faces arranged in a geometric shape. Crystals such as these should more accurately be described as 'crystalline'. This may occur, for example, when there is insufficient space for a crystal to form its perfect external shape. Alternatively, the internal structure may have many tiny crystals that are too small to be seen individually with the human eye; these can mass together to form crystalline minerals, which are specifically referred to as crypto-crystalline or poly-crystalline. A common example is rose quartz, which is most usually found in crystalline form. Other examples of crystalline materials frequently used by crystal therapists are turquoise, malachite, jadeite, carnelian

LEFT MALACHITE IS FOUND IN CRYSTALLINE PIECES. DESPITE ITS LACK OF EXTERNAL GEOMETRIC FORM, INTERNALLY IT IS QUITE REGULAR.

and jasper. Although there is no outer geometric form, the internal structure is still perfectly regular.

To further complicate the matter, crystal therapists frequently use the word 'crystal' for minerals that are not crystals at all! Often these are amorphous (meaning 'without form') minerals such as obsidian, which is a naturally occurring volcanic glass. Moldavite is another popular healing 'crystal' that is actually amorphous. It is a glass-like translucent green mineral that is formed under intense heat and pressure due to meteoritic activity and has no regular internal structure. Other popular non-crystalline minerals are 'organics' such as amber and jet, as well as coral, pearl and paua shell.

Occasionally therapists will use 'rocks' rather than crystals – for example lapis lazuli, which is an aggregate of a number of different minerals. Different minerals, including lazurite, calcite and iron pyrite, have combined together to result in this notable colour, and the flecks of gold are in fact shards of iron pyrites.

ABOVE JASPER IS AN EXAMPLE OF A CRYSTALLINE COMMONLY USED BY CRYSTAL THERAPISTS.

11

You will sometimes hear the term 'gem' used. This refers to a broad spectrum of minerals from crystals and rocks to organic products derived from once living creatures or plants.

CRYSTALS AND THE PLANET

Our 4,600 million year old planet consists largely of crystalline minerals. It is estimated that approximately 85–90 per cent of the Earth is made up of crystals. Some quartz crystals in Madagascar are thought to be around 450 million years old, having formed over a period of 200–300,000 years. Others found in Brazil are estimated to be more than 300 million years old. Crystals are therefore an ancient part of the fabric of the planet.

THE LAYERS OF THE EARTH

The planet has a radius of almost 6,500km and is made up of three main 'layers':

The crust – this is the outer layer, which lies over the surface of the planet, like a thin skin. It varies greatly in thickness from 60–70km along mountain ranges to only 6km thickness on the ocean bed.

The mantle – this is a solid layer approximately 2,900km thick that lies just below the crust.

The core – this is at the centre of the planet and consists of a molten ring or outer core that is approximately 2,000km thick, and the inner solid core, which has a radius of approximately 1,370km.

At present, physical exploration of the planet is limited to just a few kilometres into the crust – the outer layer only. Current speculation suggests that the solid inner core might be similar to a giant metallic crystal with magnetic properties. If so, this theory could support many of the current philosophies surrounding crystal therapy.

12

ABOVE THE EARTH IS COMPOSED OF THREE LAYERS – THE CRUST, THE MANTLE AND THE CORE.

How Do Crystals Form?

Crystallography – the study of crystals, their formation and scientific properties – is an immense and complex subject. However, in simple terms the process of crystallization can generally be categorized under three headings:

1. Igneous – minerals that form from molten or semi-molten rock, known as 'magma'. The magma carries a rich solution of atoms that, when conditions are right, can group together in a structured order to become crystallized. This accounts for the formation of minerals such as quartz, feldspar and olivine.

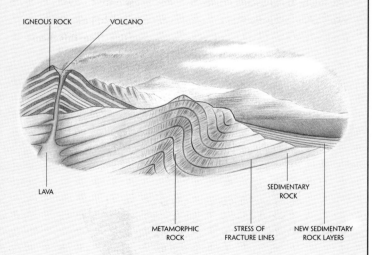

IGNEOUS ROCK   VOLCANO

LAVA

METAMORPHIC   STRESS OF   SEDIMENTARY
ROCK   FRACTURE LINES   ROCK

                                        NEW SEDIMENTARY
                                        ROCK LAYERS

ABOVE THE ROCK CYCLE IS A CONTINUAL PROCESS IN WHICH ROCKS ARE PUSHED

UP, ERODED, MOVED, COMPRESSED AND METAMORPHOSED.

2. Sedimentary – minerals that form from aqueous solution or solid pieces. Sedimentary minerals are primarily formed from water solutions or grow on or near the Earth's surface. They have nearly always been moved from their original place by natural phenomena such as waves, currents, streams or gravity. Exposure to water and the atmosphere causes layers of sediment to build up that eventually, under the pressure of accumulated weight, compresses into minerals such as sandstone.

3. Metamorphic – minerals that have their structure rearranged to cause re-crystallization. Metamorphic crystals, which were previously igneous, sedimentary or other metamorphic substances, form under great pressure and high temperatures within the Earth's crust. These undergo a natural and chemical change, often after the original formation has taken place, giving rise to a metamorphic substance. This re-crystallization process accounts for the transformation of calcite into marble. Garnet and kyanite crystals are also formed in this way.

14

LEFT GARNET IS AN EXAMPLE OF A METAMORPHIC CRYSTAL, WHICH MEANS THAT IT HAS UNDERGONE A RE-CRYSTALLIZATION PROCESS.

The formation of a crystal often involves more than one of these processes.

Crystals can stop and start growing again, as if in phases rather than in one continual flowing process. Evidence of this growing process can be seen with phantom or ghost crystals: the outline of the crystal in an earlier, and therefore smaller, stage, of its growth is shown due to a very light coating of some other mineral substance. The extraordinary colour zones seen in some tourmalines also demonstrate this growing process.

CRYSTAL MINING

All crystal mining takes place on, or very near to, the surface of the Earth. Even when seeking the most precious and sought-after of gems such as diamonds, mines rarely reach depths of more than several kilometres. When considering the proportionate depths of the crust and the remaining two layers of the Earth, it can be seen that even the most extreme mining practices barely scratch the surface of the planet.

Nevertheless, many environmentally-sensitive crystal healers are concerned about the harmful impact of utilizing crystals in their work. They fear that excessive mining may occur and that the Earth will be stripped of her crystalline treasures to the detriment of future generations.

However, as the Earth's crust is almost entirely crystalline in nature, it would be physically impossible to strip an area entirely of its crystals – that would involve removing an entire section of the Earth's crust.

Some healers feel that the mining and removal of the Earth's crystals is in fact part of a Divine plan. Their view is that the crystals of one particular area may have served their purpose energetically and are now needed in another part of the world. The most effective way of achieving this goal is for the crystals to make themselves desirable to human beings who become responsible for the logistics of moving what are essentially heavy and fragile objects over vast distances!

Perhaps of greater environmental concern are the methods of mining. Open cast mines, for example, can sometimes involve stripping the Earth's surface of trees and other vegetation. However, ethical mining practices are gradually becoming more common as public awareness is increased and environmental pressure is brought to bear on the mine owners.

15

Explosives used to play an important role in blasting crystals out of the Earth. This may be particularly the case in tourmaline mines, where large numbers of quartz crystals were also found but usually discarded as being of little commercial value. However, because of the recent new interest in quartz (largely due to crystal healing) the miners have reconsidered the amount of quartz that they are damaging and therefore unable to sell. They now employ far gentler methods of mining by hand.

Crystals can be found in veins, channels or spaces within rocks rich in crystallized deposits. These can be extracted by simply prising them loose, or, in larger-scale mining, by using drilling equipment, mechanical diggers and earth movers.

Another method of mining is to find extracts of crystalline materials such as spinels, rubies and diamonds that lie on the surface of the Earth. These are often found in stream-beds, both active and dried up, and may be part of a vein that has become exposed at some point higher up the river. The combined effects of running water and gravity have washed the crystals downstream, depositing them in areas of slower-moving water, such as on a bend, creating what is geologically known as alluvial deposits. Commonly you find miners sieving and washing gravel to separate and pick out the crystals.

Certain weather conditions, such as heavy thunderstorms, seismic activity or land slippage, may also reveal new pockets of crystals.

Sometimes it seems as if the planet monitors how many crystals may be mined and when certain varieties are made available.

It may also be of interest to note the date and location of new varieties of crystals being unearthed. For example, during the mid-1970s several previously undiscovered minerals were found. These include sugilite in South Africa, charoite in Russia and tanzanite in Tanzania.

CRYSTAL SYSTEMS

All crystals conform to one of seven specific symmetrical patterns (*see* p.18) – these patterns are known as the seven crystal systems. Crystals of one variety can only belong to one crystal system. For example, all garnets are cubic, quartz crystals are always trigonal and all topaz crystals are orthorhombic.

The systems are categorized according to degrees of symmetry. The cubic crystal system is the most symmetrical and triclinic the least symmetrical. A perfectly formed cubic crystal would resemble a cube – pyrite crystals are good examples. A perfectly formed hexagonal crystal would be a six-sided prism with flat top and bottom – beryl crystals can often be found showing this symmetry. However,

ABOVE ALL CRYSTALS FIT INTO ONE OF SEVEN CRYSTAL SYSTEMS, REFLECTING ITS INTERNAL STRUCTURE.

it is in fact fairly unusual to find a crystal perfectly displaying its crystal symmetry and for those who are unfamiliar with crystals this can be confusing! Clear quartz crystals and tourmaline crystals are two very different minerals, but both belong to the trigonal crystal system. Quartz crystals are usually six-sided with a pointed termination made up of six triangular faces, whereas tourmaline crystals are usually three-sided with a pointed termination made up of three triangular faces.

Amorphous minerals such as amber, obsidian and moldavite do not conform to any of the crystal systems as they are, by definition, without form.

LEFT AMBER HAS A FREEFORM STRUCTURE, AND IS A MINERAL NOT A CRYSTAL.

THE SEVEN CRYSTAL SYSTEMS

The seven crystal systems are as follows:

Cubic – for example, diamond, fluorite, garnet, pyrite, spinel

Tetragonal – for example, apophylite, idocrase, rutile, scapolite, zircon

Orthorhombic – for example, celestite, chrysoberyl, iolite, peridot, topaz

Monoclinic – for example, azurite, jadeite, moonstone, spodumene

Triclinic – for example, rhodonite, kyanite, labradorite, turquoise

ABOVE KYANITE IS AN EXAMPLE OF A TRICLINIC.

Hexagonal – for example, apatite, beryl, zincite

Trigonal – for example, calcite, corundum, hematite, quartz, tourmaline

Note: The American Gemmological Association refers to just six crystal systems. Trigonal and hexagonal systems are placed together under the heading of hexagonal only. However, the Gemmological Association of Great Britain teaches that these two systems are different due to the fact that the trigonal system has less symmetry than the hexagonal system.

NAMES OF CRYSTALS

As has already been discussed, therapists frequently use the word 'crystal' inaccurately to refer to non-crystalline minerals such as obsidian and amber. The words 'stone', 'gem' and 'rock' as well as 'crystal' are often used interchangeably to refer to any mineral that a therapist might employ for healing. Although this is not correct in geological and gemmological terms, in healing circles it is now a commonly accepted practice.

The individual names of crystals can cause much confusion. The same crystal may have several names depending upon its colour, value, quality and marketability. For example, sugilite is also known as lovulite and royal azul – same mineral, three different names!

Frequently, the raw, unworked material will have one name and high-grade jewellery quality another. Olivine is the name of the green mineral more commonly known as peridot when used in jewellery. It therefore has to be of sufficiently good colour and transparency to be classified as gem-quality.

Some crystals are grouped under family or group names. For example, corundum is the family or group name of which the blue high- or gem-quality corundum is more often referred to as sapphire – gem-quality red corundum is simply referred to as ruby. A further example of this is the beryl family or group, which includes aquamarine, emerald and morganite.

19

CRYSTAL FAMILIES

The following is a list of the more common crystal families:

1. BERYL
Different varieties of beryl are known by different names – blue is aquamarine, yellow is heliodor, pink is morganite, colourless or

brown is goshenite, green is emerald, and red is bixbite (also known as red beryl).

2. CORUNDUM

Red corundum is more commonly known as ruby and the blue variety as sapphire. Both ruby and sapphire have exactly the same chemical composition, but traces of different elements cause the different colour e.g. chromium for ruby, and iron and titanium for sapphire. Yellow and pink sapphires also exist.

ABOVE EMERALD BELONGS TO THE BERYL FAMILY.

LEFT RUBY IS THE COMMON NAME FOR THE RED VARIETY OF THE CORUNDUM.

3. FELDSPARS

This is a very large group of minerals, the most well known of which is moonstone. Other minerals in this group often used by crystal therapists are labradorite, sunstone and amazonite. To add to the confusion, not all feldspars are part of the same crystal system. For example, moonstone is monoclinic but labradorite is triclinic.

ABOVE THE POPULAR MOONSTONE CRYSTAL BELONGS TO THE FELDSPAR FAMILY.

4. GARNET

There are many different varieties of garnet that occur in a range of colours. Some of the more well known are: almandine, a burgundy red to brownish colour, pyrope, which is red, spessartine, a yellowish orange to reddish brown and demantoid, which is bright green.

5. QUARTZ

This family includes clear quartz (also known as rock crystal), as well as rose quartz, amethyst, citrine, smoky quartz and all the jaspers, agates, aventurine and onyx.

6. TOURMALINE

Members of this family are found in many colours and combinations of colours. Colourless tourmaline is known as achroite, black as schorl, rose red as rubellite, green as verdelite and blue to blue green as indicolite. Watermelon tourmaline refers to tourmaline that has a pink inner core and green on the outside.

ABOVE VERDELITE, A GREEN TOURMALINE.

7. ZOISITE

Members of the zoisite family include tanzanite, a blue or blue violet tri-coloured gem variety and thulite (the international stone of Norway), which is pinkish. There is also a green variety that is simply known as zoisite. In India this green zoisite is often found as the matrix rock (i.e. mother or surrounding mineral) for ruby crystals.

Other confusing names include jade. There are two distinct varieties of jade, nephrite and jadeite. Jade is merely the collective name for both types. Most people believe that jade only occurs in various shades of green, but it can be found in many different colours including yellow and purple, although these are less common. Also, kunzite and hiddenite are two differently coloured varieties of the mineral, spodumene. Generally, kunzite is pink and hiddenite is green. Gypsum and selenite are the same mineral. 'Fishtail selenite' is not mineralogically different, but refers to the particular way the crystal has formed.

THE "MYSTICAL" PROPERTIES OF CRYSTALS

There are various theories that attempt to explain the extraordinary healing powers of crystals. However, it is up to each individual to explore what they feel to be their personal truth and arrive at their own conclusions. Ideally, first experience for yourself the healing energies that crystals can impart and then begin to develop a sense of what is happening and find an explanation that works for you. Then be prepared to change your mind! As you work more with crystals, your understanding will deepen and new insights will occur to you. We recommend that you let the crystals be your teachers. However, to get you started, we have detailed below some of the more popular ideas and theories:-

PATTERNS OF PERFECTION

Crystals are physical patterns of perfection. Their harmonious internal atomic structures and geometric external forms give humans a perfect template to emulate. Crystals can tune us into a greater degree of perfection. In the same way that singers might use a tuning fork to help them sing together perfectly in tune, humans can use crystals to become inspired by their perfection and to attain balance and harmony, and, ultimately, good health.

SOURCES OF INSPIRATION

Looking at beautiful landscapes in nature and works of art or listening to sacred and moving music can open our hearts and minds, helping us to feel inspired, relaxed and healed. Crystals have a natural and breathtaking beauty that works in the same way. As we become inspired, we are more able to connect to a universal healing source that helps us to become whole and balanced.

MINERAL CONTENT AND COLOUR

There are many therapeutic arts that draw upon the healing vibrations of colour and a simple but popular explanation for the healing powers of crystals is their bright and vibrant colours – they literally display 'jewel-like' colours.

Healing therapists such as homeopaths and nutritionists emphasize the need for a correct balance of minerals for good health. Some healers feel that by holding a crystal it is able to impart, at a vibrationary level, tiny amounts of the various parts of its mineral composition to bring about balance and health in an individual. For example, turquoise includes some copper in its chemical composition, peridot contains iron, some tourmalines are rich in lithium and some garnets contain magnesium.

RIGHT THE VIBRATIONAL HEALING QUALITIES OF A CRYSTAL MAY BE RELEASED THROUGH TOUCH.

23

THE HUMAN CRYSTAL

Many parts of the human body are crystalline in nature. One example is the apatite crystals that are found in our bones and teeth. Current research is now showing that many parts of the body and its systems have similar patterns to crystals. It could be suggested that there is a recognition and resonance between the inorganic earth crystals and the organic 'bio' crystals of the human body. Because of this resonance, the human body is particularly receptive to the healing properties that crystals can offer.

SENSE OF PERSPECTIVE

Crystals are an intrinsic part of the history of the human race. Throughout the ages, crystals have been revered as mysterious and sacred talismans. They have been considered magical tools for healing and symbols of power and authority. They are very old – crystals predate even the earliest human civilizations by many millions of years. These factors serve to remind us humans of our fragile and short lives on this planet. In other words, crystals can help to restore our sense of perspective, which in itself can be a healing process.

CRYSTAL GEOMETRY AND FORM

Crystals could be described as living geometric symbols. They display an extraordinary natural geometry that is reminiscent of many archetypal healing symbols. For example, the six-armed star is a formation that can be found in rose quartz, the square or cube is very clearly seen in fluorite crystals and triangles can be seen as etch marks in diamonds and in tourmaline crystals.

PHYSICAL PROPERTIES OF CRYSTALS

Crystals have a number of physical properties that have been utilized by industry. For example, silicon chips are used in computers and ruby crystals are used in lasers. Perhaps these physical attributes also help to explain the healing properties of crystals.

As white light passes through a crystal several things occur. The light is 'dispersed' into the seven spectrum colours – Isaac Newton (1642–1727) used a quartz crystal prism to demonstrate the phenomena of dispersion. The light is refracted, i.e. slowed down and the angle changed. Many crystals at the same time also polarize the light. Most coloured and some clear crystals will absorb parts of the spectrum.

RIGHT A PRISM BENDS COLOURS IN WHITE LIGHT BY DIFFERENT AMOUNTS, PRODUCING A RANGE OF COLOURS.

Many healers talk about channelling 'light' when they are giving healing. Most patterns in the universe seem to repeat at higher and lower levels. It might be reasonable, therefore, to assume that, if crystals affect physical light so significantly, they will also affect healing light vibrations. As healing energy is channelled through a crystal perhaps it is filtered and specifically shaped by the crystal, thereby emphasizing specific parts of the spectrum. Possibly the healing vibration is subtly altered as it passes through the crystal, the speed and direction being changed by the presence of the crystal, the resulting light patterns forming sacred geometric shapes such as the equi-distant cross.

Tourmaline is both pyro-electric and piezo-electric, which means when a crystal is either heated (pyro) or subjected to pressure (piezo) it produces an electric reaction. Perhaps this electrical charge is also created as a response to the stimulus of healing energy. Some crystal therapists lightly tap or squeeze their crystals to help produce a healing vibration.

25

Many crystals have other physical properties. Some are magnetic. Others are fluorescent, reacting to ultra-violet light. This connection between the healing properties and the physical properties of crystals is an area that is only just beginning to be explored. There is still a great deal to discover about crystals and their extraordinary healing powers.

THE HISTORY OF CRYSTAL THERAPY

CHAPTER TWO

Since the earliest of times people have been attracted by the natural beauty, magic and mystery of crystals. This deep fascination has led civilizations, ancient and modern, to revere crystals both for their practical uses and their mystical or healing qualities.

Myths and legends speak of touchstones, magical amulets, talismans and crystal balls. Mythical heroes carry gem-encrusted swords and shields. Heads of state and religions use magnificent gems as symbols of power, wealth and authority. In addition, specific gemstones, such as the Koh-I-Noor diamond, have become legendary or infamous.

MYTHS AND LEGENDS

Crystals have been used throughout the ages for their supposed magical properties, including as an aid to divination.

Rings in particular have been noticeable throughout history and are often connected with 'magic' or 'powers'. King Solomon was said to have worn a ring that had been given to him by the angels. The setting was made of brass and iron, the metals of Venus and Mars. This meant that Solomon could be helped by the good spirits commanded by Venus and control the evil spirits by Martian iron influence.

The Ancient Greeks thought of quartz crystal as frozen water. When they found that they could create fire by directing the sun's rays through quartz, they attributed mystical powers beyond measure to this wondrous stone.

To be able to create fire from frozen water was deemed to be one of the great mysteries in ancient philosophy. Quartz was therefore greatly revered; only priests were allowed to use the crystals to create the sacred fire.

ABOVE THE ANCIENT GREEKS ATTRIBUTED MYSTICAL POWERS TO QUARTZ CRYSTAL .

27

THE KOH-I-NOOR DIAMOND

The Koh-I-Noor diamond (meaning mountain of light) has the longest history of all the famous diamonds and has been traced back as far as 1304.

It probably originated in India and eventually came to Queen Victoria, who had it re-cut from its original 280 carats to 108.93 carats. It was set into the crown of Queen Elizabeth II and is now a part of the British Crown Jewels.

One superstition states that it will bring great misfortune to any man who wears it, but not to a woman.

The Moguls believed that whoever owned this stone would rule the whole world.

It was also said that the water in which this diamond is placed would cure any disease.

CRYSTAL SKULLS

Crystal skulls are surrounded by numerous myths and legends. There is much discussion between experts regarding the origins, age and manufacturing methods used to create these extraordinary and beautiful objects.

The workmanship displayed by some of the skulls is extremely skilled and sophisticated; some even have a moveable jaw. However, others are cruder symbolic representations of the human skull.

Legends say the skulls are able to talk or sing. Thirteen crystal skulls are said to exist, although some may still remain undiscovered. When the human race has evolved to a sufficiently high moral and spiritual plane, then, legend says, the skulls will make available their collective wisdom.

Other legends say that the skulls were brought to earth from another plane of existence (or possibly Atlantis) to help humanity in their great time of need. The skulls are to help us remember the past and to create a meaningful future, reminding us that we are spiritual beings in physical bodies.

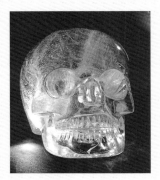

ABOVE THE CHANGING COLOURS WITHIN A CRYSTAL SKULL MIRRORED THE NEED TO LIVE IN HARMONY WITH THE ENERGIES OF THE UNIVERSE.

One of the most renowned legends that surround crystals relates to the ancient lost civilization of Atlantis. Whether Atlantis actually existed or is merely a myth is still the subject of much debate.

It is said that crystals powered the great civilization of Atlantis and it was the abuse of this power that led to its downfall. According to Edgar Cayce (1877–1945), the use of crystals played an important role in Atlantis as a means of Divine communication. Large reflective crystals were at first used for spiritual communication between the infinite and finite. As time progressed, crystals became used as generators, radiating power and energy across the land without using wires. A central crystal rested in the temple called 'The Temple of the Sun in Poseida', which was a central power station. Covered by a stone, it was exposed, as needed, to the sun's rays. As the rays shone onto the crystal, its energy was harnessed, magnified and intensified by many prisms. Such was the crystal's power that it could be transmitted and regenerated throughout the land. Beamed as radio waves, it powered cities, ships and aircraft. Cayce goes on to say that even the human body, when exposed to a small amount of this energy, could be rejuvenated.

ANCIENT CIVILIZATIONS

Flint tools have been found in many ancient sites. This suggests that flint, which is a variety of quartz, has played an important part in the lives of humans for more than two million years. Flint was used to help create fire, which was considered the most precious, magical and powerful resource of all.

Archaeological studies have shown that crystals in the form of colourful opaque pebbles were used in 25,000 BC as forms of adornment and decoration. They may also have had symbolic significance, possibly in terms of tribal seniority and wealth or possibly talismanic properties. Their discovery in burial chambers, mounds and caves suggests that they were valued possessions.

RIGHT THE ANCESTORS OF MODERN HUMANS USED FLINT TO FASHION THE FIRST TOOLS.

In Somerset, England, recent archaeological excavations have discovered the body of a Stone Age woman. Buried with her was a polished sphere of crystalline granite. Archaeologists believe that the sphere may have been a revered magical instrument that enabled her to have visions or some form of Divine insight.

Dark stone bowls have been found throughout the world. When filled with water, these become like mirrors and may have been used by shamans, seers and healers to gain insight and as meditation tools. These objects may have been early forerunners to the crystal ball, which has been used for scrying (crystal gazing) for the last five or six centuries.

By 7,000 BC in civilizations such as the Sumerians, crystals such as carnelian and clear quartz were being made into cylindrical seals, which were used to mark property and became popular as talismans.

The Ancient Egyptians made much use of crystals. Lapis lazuli, which had been mined in Afghanistan and transported to Egypt, has been found in tombs that date back to 5,000 BC. In the same era, turquoise was being mined in the Sinai and again used by the Egyptians. These crystals were used by the priests to make statues of their ancient gods and goddesses.

Reincarnation and the journey into the after-life was fundamental to the Egyptian belief system. Crystals including amethyst, lapis lazuli, emerald and carnelian have been recovered from the tombs of the pharaohs. They were placed over the heart, or carved into a stylized eye to watch over the soul as it journeyed into the after-life. Carnelian was considered to represent the process of reincarnation and thought

ABOVE THE ANCIENT EGYPTIANS USED TURQUOISE TO DECORATE THEIR RELIGIOUS IMAGES.

to protect against the evils that might be encountered as the soul passed through into the underworld. The Egyptian papyrus *Ebers* dated 1600 BC refers to various medicinal uses for crystals. For example, lapis lazuli for cataracts, emeralds to help dysentery, amethyst as a snakebite antidote, sapphires for eye diseases and rubies to help liver and spleen disorders.

The ancient Greeks were the first to record the medicinal healing applications of crystals formally in depth. Theophrastus (372–287 BC) wrote the oldest surviving mineralogical text. Entitled *On Stones*, it examined 16 minerals for their physical geological properties and medical values.

The magnetic properties of lodestone were discovered in ancient Greece and it was recommended that this crystal be rubbed onto the surface of the skin – presumably to draw out any pain or impurities. This use of lodestone might be considered the earliest example of magnetic therapy, which is at the present time enjoying something of a revival.

31

The Roman writer, Pliny the Elder (AD 23–79) produced a significant written work relating to the healing properties of crystals, called *Historia Naturalis*. This work, which consisted of 37 volumes, detailed over a thousand facts, romantic stories and scientific observations concerning gems. The *Historia* was a major influence until medieval times.

In the first century AD, the Roman writer Pedanius Dioscorides wrote his *De Materia Medica*. The fifth volume listed more than 200 stones, together with their therapeutic properties. Recipes included the use of powdered agate, which was mixed with sweet fruit as a treatment for insanity, ulcers and kidney problems. This is a treatment that today's crystal therapists would definitely not recommend! Dioscorides' work became a physician's reference book for more than 1,600 years.

Crystals have also played an integral part in many of the world's religions. In Buddhist traditions there are seven precious metals and gems that are spiritually revered: gold, silver, sapphires or rubies,

cat's eyes, diamonds, corals and pearls. Pope Gregory the Great
(c. AD 540–604) was said to have assigned a gemstone to each order
of ascending angels, with emerald given to the highest. The wearer of
such gems was believed to then attract the associated angelic order.
Tibetans used turquoise in healing ceremonies because they believed
it could help to draw out illness from the body.

THE BREASTPLATE OF JUDGEMENT

**The High Priest's Breastplate, which is also sometimes known as the
Breastplate of Judgement, is referred to in Exodus in the Old
Testament. It resembled the upper body garment the Greeks wore in
battle. Encrusted with 12 differently coloured and positioned stones,
it was said to be divinely inspired and have limitless spiritual
powers. Some believe it to represent the emblem of the 12 signs of
the zodiac, with each stone representing a special significance
according to ancient philosophy.**

THE MIDDLE AGES UP TO THE 19TH CENTURY

In medieval times there were many alchemist physicians who
promoted the use of crystals for a variety of healing applications,
ranging from a treatment for the plague to an antidote to venom.

Many Crusaders wore a red garnet either as a ring, in a buckle or on
their sword or shield, as it was thought that garnets had magical
properties to slow the flow of blood. Surgeons would place a stone on
a wound or haemorrhage. Throughout the ages, many soldiers from
all over the world have considered garnet to be a stone of protection
and victory, and even today it is thought that some soldiers in the
Middle East still carry a garnet in some guise.

THE HISTORY OF CRYSTAL THERAPY

Physicians from the 1300s to the 1600s believed that rubies promoted both mental and physical health. John Manderville, in the 1300s, recorded that the owner of a ruby would be granted peacefulness and a tranquil life.

The 13th century explorer Marco Polo encountered many crystals on his travels and was obviously fascinated by this subject. He wrote travel books, which included reference to crystals and their healing properties and legends. He writes of his visits to the lapis lazuli mines in Afghanistan, 'fishing for pearls' and 'gathering turquoises'. Like many scholars in the 13th century, the German philosopher, Albert Magnus, wrote about minerals and he noted the magical properties of 94 different minerals.

In the 1600s, physic William Roland prepared medicines using garnet. He believed garnet would aid heart problems by stimulating the heart, improving the flow of blood and reducing melancholy. In the 17th century the court physician to the Holy Roman Emperor, Rudolf II, wrote an extensive work describing gems and their powers.

33

THE 20TH CENTURY

Crystal therapy is not a product of the New Age, although interest has grown steadily since the early 1970s. At the beginning of the 20th century, a number of books describing the metaphysical properties of crystals were published, including *The Curious Lore of Precious Stones* by George Frederick Kunz (1913).

In the mid-1970s there was a strong upsurge of interest in crystals coinciding with a general increase of interest in spiritual matters and complementary medicine. Many books were published on the subject, and teachers started to emerge and by the 1980s, a number of people were trying to find formal training for crystal therapists.

In Great Britain the Affiliation of Crystal Healing Organizations (ACHO) was formed in 1988 by a small group of crystal healing organizations. ACHO aims to support and promote crystal therapists.

NATIVE AMERICANS AND SHAMANISM

The Native Americans are renowned crystal therapists. The Cherokee specialize in using crystal wands in their work with crystals. The Arizona Hopi use crystals to gaze at the energy centres, also known as the chakras, which are situated along the spine, in order to assess their health levels. Native American shamans, like many medicine men and women worldwide, frequently carry small pouches, known as medicine bags, and invariably these will include some crystals and stones.

There is also a Native American myth that says that various parts of the mineral realm represent parts of the planet's body system. The precious gems of the world such as rubies, diamonds and emeralds, symbolize the organs of the planet, and for this reason it is important to look at the geographical location of major sources of precious gems. Quartz crystals, which are found worldwide, are the brain cells that contain the memories of the entire planet's history. The earth's rocks represent the bones and skeleton of the planet, and the sands symbolize the skin.

The Huichol Indians in Central Mexico believe that when a shaman dies his or her soul will eventually return to the earth in the form of a quartz crystal. The Warao shamans in South America put quartz crystals into their medicine rattles because they believe the crystals to be helpers in spirit form who can help to remove negativity and invasive energy from the body.

LEFT CRYSTAL WANDS PLAY A SIGNIFICANT PART IN THE HEALING RITUALS OF MANY CHEROKEE MEDICINE MEN.

Nationally recognized training standards have been established, involving a minimum training period of two years.

Although crystal therapy is still not recognized as a mainstream therapy in the way that homeopathy or aromatherapy are accepted, it is becoming more widely known. Most members of the general public have heard of crystal therapy even if they are not sure what it entails. Crystal therapy is regularly featured in newspaper and magazine articles, and the ACHO receives a steady stream of enquiries for names of practitioners as well as details of how to train as a crystal therapist. There is no doubt that crystals fascinate us just as much today as they did thousands of years ago.

CRYSTAL THERAPY IN THE FUTURE

As we start the new millennium, it seems that health issues are being viewed from a much wider perspective, and interest in all forms of vibrational healing continues to grow. Crystal therapy is currently attracting interest from nurses and doctors, as well as practitioners who are already trained in other forms of complementary therapy. This would seem to suggest that there is a desire for a more spiritual and holistic approach to healing. Perhaps we will go back to our roots and look at how the planet and its crystal resources can help to support us back to a whole and healthy future.

35

APPLYING CRYSTAL THERAPY

CHAPTER THREE

If you would like to receive crystal therapy treatment, it is important to take some time to find the right practitioner. Most therapists will be happy to have a brief telephone conversation with you, during which they can provide outline information about their qualifications, how they work, how long they have been in practice, whether or not they are insured and what you might expect during a session. At the same time, establish practical details such as length of sessions and how much a treatment costs. Also, find out if the practitioner is a member of an organization that requires him or her to adhere to a code of conduct.

WHAT HAPPENS DURING A CRYSTAL HEALING TREATMENT?

There is no set procedure for a consultation because every therapist works in their own unique way. However, most consultations include some of the elements set out below.

The session will usually begin with a discussion. The therapist may explain about the therapy and this could be a good time for you to ask any questions. Some therapists like to take a detailed case history and will include questions about lifestyle, diet and exercise

TRAINING AS A CRYSTAL THERAPIST

If you are considering training as a crystal therapist, you may wish to explore the philosophy of your chosen training organization to ensure that it corresponds with your own belief system and feels right for you. Find out how long the training organization has been established and the level of experience of the tutors. If formal accreditation is offered, clarify what qualifications you will gain, what practitioner registers you can join, if recognition is national or international and who is the formal lead body or examining body. You may also wish to find out about on-going support after you have qualified, such as further training opportunities and therapist supervision.

as well as a full medical history and details of any medication being taken. At subsequent sessions, a little time is spent at the beginning to discuss how you have felt since the last session and what, if anything, has changed or developed. All case records are confidential to you and the therapist.

Crystal therapy is suitable for everyone regardless of age or health. However, certain adaptations are necessary for clients with high blood pressure, epilepsy or those with a pacemaker. Also, special care is taken with pregnant women and young children, who may be especially sensitive to crystals.

RIGHT IT IS IMPORTANT TO FEEL AT EASE WITH YOUR THERAPIST SO THAT YOU CAN BUILD A GOOD RAPPORT.

Your therapist may ask you to lie down on a couch or sit on a chair. Others prefer to work on the floor. However, it is important that you feel comfortable so do not be afraid to state your preferences.

Generally, unless the session is to also include another therapy such as an aromatherapy body massage, you will remain fully clothed, but you may be asked to remove shoes and loosen any articles of tight clothing. Some therapists may also ask you to remove watches and jewellery, particularly crystal jewellery, as they feel it may interfere with the flow of energy. Some therapists like to play relaxing music. Others may lead you through a guided visualization to help you relax.

Your therapist may ask you to hold one or two crystals. He or she may place crystals on your body or around you, or they could be placed beneath the chair or massage couch. The therapist may also be holding crystals. The crystals can be left in place for just a few seconds or throughout the whole session. Just a few crystals may be used or a complex pattern consisting of many crystals can be created. Even if you are experiencing physical pains or symptoms, the therapist will not necessarily place a crystal on this particular part of your body. Crystal therapy is a holistic treatment and the therapist will work at a much broader level and may well be treating the cause of the problem, which could be located in another part of your body or subtle energy field.

Some therapists will ask you at the beginning of the session to pick out a crystal that attracts you and they may use this during the treatment. Often the crystals will feel cold or heavy

ABOVE AT SOME CONSULTATIONS YOU WILL BE ASKED TO PICK OUT A CRYSTAL – THIS WILL THEN BE USED IN YOUR TREATMENT.

when they are first placed on you. However, after a few minutes you will probably get used to them. You may even become unaware that you are holding crystals – it is as if they dissolve into your hands and your body – or they may become very warm and comforting. However, if you experience discomfort or pain at any time during the session, be sure to inform your therapist.

Most people find a crystal therapy session a relaxing and pleasant experience. If you have never experienced any form of complementary medicine before, you may find it difficult to relax for the first couple of sessions. However, this usually improves with time as you become more familiar with the process and your therapist.

During the treatment you may be vaguely aware of your therapist moving around you, placing and removing crystals or gently stroking them through your energy field without touching you. You may occasionally feel warmth or tingling or even a slight cool breeze on your skin. Occasionally it is possible to experience what is sometimes described as a 'healing crisis', which usually involves a slight worsening of physical symptoms for a few hours. This is normally considered a positive sign and usually precedes an improvement in the condition. It is also possible to feel a little emotional and weepy after the healing has taken place. These effects can occur during or immediately after the session or two or three days later. It is common to feel especially tired for a few hours after a session and we recommend that our clients try to arrange to have a quiet evening and an early night after having crystal therapy. If you are concerned at all after a session you should not hesitate to consult with your therapist to gain guidance.

At the end of the treatment your therapist will remove any crystals and gently encourage you to become more alert and consciously aware of your surroundings. You may feel like you are being woken up after a brief nap. In fact, some clients fall asleep during their session. Your therapist will always ensure that you are fully grounded and awake before leaving to travel home. If you do not feel sufficiently awake and alert, please tell your therapist.

Some therapists will give you a crystal to take home with you so that you can continue your crystal therapy. They may also give you a crystal elixir (*see* below) or arrange to send you distant healing (*see* pp.42–45).

The number of sessions required by different patients will, of course, vary greatly but review this with your therapist on a regular basis. We recommend to our healers that they leave intervals of at least one week between sessions as it can take several days for the effects of the treatment to unfold. As a guide, we would suggest that you should feel some benefits from the therapy after three sessions. If you do not feel that you have gained anything positive from the three sessions, we would strongly urge you to review whether crystal therapy, or the chosen therapist, is the best option for you at this time.

GEM ELIXIRS

Gem elixirs are also called crystal or gem essences, or crystal or gem remedies. Occasionally, they are called gem or crystal tinctures.

Some crystal therapists prefer to use crystal elixirs in their treatments rather than crystals in their solid form. Other therapists supplement their use of crystals with gem elixirs. For example, they may give their client an elixir to take home, which then can be used between sessions, or a few drops of an elixir may be given to the patient at the end of the therapy session.

ABOVE A GEM ELIXIR CONTAINS THE HEALING ENERGY OF THE CRYSTAL OR CRYSTALS USED TO MAKE IT.

In simple terms, a gem elixir is water that has been imbued with the healing qualities of a crystal or crystals. An elixir can be made by placing a crystal in a glass of water and leaving it in sunlight for at least a few hours in order to allow the crystal's 'energetic signature' – in other words, its healing properties – to imprint the water.

Some therapists suggest leaving the crystal in the water overnight and drinking the crystal-charged water the next morning. Other therapists like to channel or pulse (by tapping or squeezing the crystal) a healing energy through the crystal, which is held above the glass of water. Alternatively, they may hold the glass of water in one hand and the crystal in the other. Then, via a process sometimes known as 'triangulation', the energy of the crystal is passed through the therapist into the water.

You may wish to make your own elixir, in which case please exercise some caution as some crystals are potentially harmful (*see* pp.76–77) Others may be water-soluble or could fragment in water. Most crystals from the quartz family are considered safe enough to

ABOVE TO MAKE AN ELIXIR, PUT A CRYSTAL IN A PLAIN GLASS BOWL, ADD SPRING WATER AND PLACE IN THE SUNLIGHT.

41

place in the water, which is later drunk. However, these should be thoroughly washed in warm soapy water first of all to remove any potentially toxic residues left over from the mining processes. We would recommend that you choose crystals with smooth surfaces such as natural quartz crystals or pieces that have been tumbled. Avoid any crystal pieces that might fragment such as chunks of rose quartz.

Crystal elixirs can be applied in a number of ways. During a healing session, a few drops may be placed on the chakras or key points of the body. A few drops may be placed on the hands of the therapist who then brushes through the aura. Sometimes the elixirs are in small remedy bottles that are placed on or around the body in exactly the same way as crystals.

The client may take home a bottle of an elixir that has been prepared with his or her specific needs in mind and may involve a combination of several crystals. This elixir can be taken orally or may be rubbed into the skin on pulse points, chakras and, if appropriate, the area of pain. Drops of elixir can also be placed in the bath, added to aromatherapy oils or sprayed into a room – all with good effect.

Elixirs are not only effective for humans, animals and plants also

respond well to this form of vibrational healing. A few drops of the elixir can be added to the animal's food or water or rubbed onto its coat. Plants may benefit from some crystal elixir being added to their water or sprayed onto their foliage.

LEFT KEEP YOUR HOUSEPLANTS IN GOOD HEALTH BY ADDING GEM ELIXIR TO THEIR WATER OR BY SPRAYING THEIR LEAVES WITH THE ELIXIR.

DISTANT HEALING WITH CRYSTALS

Distant healing, which may also be referred to as 'absent healing', is a technique that can be employed when the patient and healer are unable to meet physically in the same place. It is simply another form of crystal therapy that should be considered and, if appropriate, added to the therapist's repertoire of healing techniques.

The effects of distant healing can be remarkable and in no way should it be considered as an inferior method, as some healers might suggest.

Most therapists like to have a physical representation of the energy of the patient. This is known as a 'witness' and can come in various forms. We recommend a photograph of the patient, preferably full length without any images of other people or animals, who may otherwise also receive healing energy. However, a witness can also be an item of jewellery, the patient's signature, a lock of hair, a treasured possession or, of course, a personal crystal that has been worked with by the patient and has been imbued with their energy.

There are many differing theories regarding how distant healing 'works' and how healing energy can, in some cases, be transferred over entire continents. One of the simplest theories, and one that we personally favour, is that the whole planet is inter-connected. The world as we know it is constructed of countless billions of atoms and electrons all bound together in various frequencies that manifest as different substances. In simple terms, a solid brick wall is made up of the very same basic building blocks that create water. In fact there is no such thing as empty space because the very air that we breathe is also made up of atoms and electrons that are all connected to each other. It is through this vast network or weave of energy that totally surrounds and supports us that energy passes. In much the same way as sunlight is able to pass through the atmosphere, so too can healing energy. The only difference is that we intend for that energy to be directed to a specific person and we work along the premise that energy follows thought.

There is one issue that we feel every conscientious therapist should address. Permission of the patient should be obtained before distant healing is sent. Although it is possible to send healing to anyone anywhere and at any time, we would question the ethics of such actions. We feel that every person has the right to make a choice and healing should be invited, not imposed. However, obtaining the permission of the patient may not always be possible. If the patient is unconscious or only a baby, permission may be given by a guardian, next-of-kin, close friend or relative. Owners or guardians of animals can similarly grant permission. In addition to

43

ELECTRO-CRYSTAL THERAPY

Electro-crystal therapy is a fascinating 20th century discovery that has been pioneered by Harry Oldfield. He combines the use of Western technology with Eastern traditions to form a modern-day healing technique.

Harry Oldfield has been experimenting with electromagnetism and its use in healing for some years. He is one of the few people today working in this field who is able to give scientific evidence of his methods and a record of his results. He videos the auric field and records it on computer disk. The computer utilizes a special programme that analyses light coming off a person. The pictures seen are like those heat pictures that we see on the weather forecast of the world. A broad outline of the body is seen with differing patches of colour around it. The various coloured areas that can be seen indicate the energy of an individual at that time.

It was discovered that a pure electromagnetic field used with relaxing and stimulating frequencies, but without crystals, produced a good effect on pain and inflammation. However, the healing spectrum dramatically increased when appropriate crystals were used. Properties of crystals such as quartz, topaz, agates or tourmaline are utilized. A special flexible silicon tube contains a conductive liquid with a crystal placed inside, an electromagnetic generator then stimulates the crystal. This causes the crystals to emit enhanced vibrations.

The human body vibrates at its own unique frequency. If one part of the body is out of alignment or out of synchronicity with the whole, it vibrates at a different frequency to the rest. The aim of electro-crystal therapy is to pick out the area in dis-harmony and try to stimulate or calm the person's subtle field to bring it into balance.

44

this, extra time should be spent in meditation and prayer to establish that the healing masters are happy for us to represent their energy in this manner.

USING CRYSTALS TO SUPPORT OTHER THERAPIES

Many therapists and teachers are discovering their own unique ways of combining their other talents and skills with the incredible powers of crystals. The therapists mentioned in this section can be contacted for more information and a list of their books can also be found at the end of the book (*see* Useful Addresses, pp.122–124 and Further Reading, p.121).

Sue and Simon Lilly, principals of the Institute of Crystal and Gem Therapists, have developed a system of using crystals called 'energy nets'. Some of the nets draw upon astrological principles and relate to specific planets, and others harness the energies of the five elements.

45

Hazel Raven, principal of the International Association of Crystal Healing Therapists, incorporates some of the principles of yoga into her courses. She teaches her students *pranayama*, a breathing exercise, as a way of helping to set up a resonance with the crystal energies. She feels that an understanding of the ancient knowledge and spiritual wisdom that comes from the study of yoga enhances and combines powerfully with the crystalline frequencies.

Sue Richter, principal of the Academy of Crystal and Natural Healing, uses crystals with Feng Shui. Feng Shui is the Chinese art of arranging our surroundings in a

LEFT ACCORDING TO THE CHINESE ART OF FENG SHUI, PLACING A CRYSTAL IN A STRATEGIC POSITION WILL ENHANCE POSITIVE ENERGY.

harmonious way. This can involve rearranging our home or work setting. Strategic placement of mirrors, plants or lead glass crystals can bring good luck. For example, quartz crystals are able to change the *chi* (life force) in a room – its flow can be enhanced, calmed down or speeded up.

Ivy Smith, principal of the Academy of Crystal Enlightenment, includes within her syllabus the topic of the spiritual evolution of the human crystalline body. She teaches her students how to create multi-dimensional crystal patterns, which re-align and purify the human crystalline body in order to create a purer channel through which spiritual energy may be directed. As humans evolve and are able to channel higher frequencies of healing light, so a purer vibration will fill the planet.

Jacquie Burgess is a psychotherapist and counsellor who uses crystals in her work. A very powerful technique she uses is the walking or journeying through the 'spiral of nine'. A visible spiral is marked out on the ground. Then nine crystals (quartz points) are strategically placed from the centre outwards at various places on the compass points. The person then walks into the centre anti-clockwise and back out in a clockwise direction. This is a powerful and moving technique only to be tried by someone with appropriate training. It can be a journey of life and if used appropriately can help people face fears and unlock them.

Past life regression is another popular therapy. Marion Webb de Sisto brings certain crystals into the regression environment in order to enhance and focus the

LEFT CRYSTALS MAY BE PLACED AROUND A PATIENT UNDERGOING PAST LIFE REGRESSION.

process. A client may be asked to hold a crystal during a session while other small clusters or tumble stones are placed around them. Several clients who have received regression therapy with and without the aid of the mineral realm have reported a preference for sessions with crystals. They described their experiences as being more easily accessed, having greater intensity and increased visual input, yet not leaving them with any leftover feelings of trauma after the completion of a session.

Chloe Asprey brings crystals into her work as a shamanic teacher. Her 'living sculptures', which incorporate crystals and symbols from the plant and animal realms, are helping to bring shamanism into the modern world. Crystals also play their part in medicine wheels, medicine bags and shamanic rituals. Shamanism teaches that everything is interconnected, and that nothing lives in isolation. The discipline of working with crystals and the process of cleansing and dedicating helps also to keep the therapist cleansed and focused.

HOW CRYSTALS AFFECT THE HUMAN BODY

CHAPTER FOUR

Human beings are made up of much more than just a physical body. There also exists a complex, subtle anatomical structure, which is particularly sensitive to any kind of vibrational medicine such as crystal therapy. When healing energy is channelled through or combined with crystals, the crystals can act as filters that specifically shape the energy that is directed towards the patient. Crystals can direct and pulsate energy into a particular part of the energy system, or they can absorb and draw out excess or negative vibrations. They can also act as a bridge or link between two points as well as amplifying and magnifying energy. Crystals naturally carry other physical properties such as colour, shape and minerals, which are also imparted during the healing process.

Crystals support the whole energy system of both the crystal therapist and the patient. The natural healing vibrations of the crystals will begin to work simply by introducing the correct crystals into the energy field of the therapist and patient. This will enable the therapist to channel more effectively and the patient to be more open and receptive to the healing.

THE CHAKRA SYSTEM

The chakra system is a widely recognized subtle energy system, referred to by many esoteric traditions and accepted as an integral part of most complementary therapies. The chakra system has primarily Indian and Eastern origins, and most complementary practitioners will include a study of the chakras in their training. Many crystal therapists work specifically on the chakras, finding crystals to be very effective in these areas.

The word *chakra* is a Sanskrit word meaning 'wheel'. The seven major chakras, also sometimes called 'energy centres', are located along the central core of the body, from the top of the head to the base of the spine. In addition, there are numerous minor chakras located throughout the body, for example, in the palms of the hands, soles of the feet and in the knees and hips. Chakras are positioned on points of the body where there is a concentration or crossover of energy or life force. Each of the main chakras traditionally has specific functions, characteristics and correspondences to certain organs, glands and senses within the body.

49

Chakras are like vortices of energy. It can be helpful to think of a chakra as a very flexible cone made up of an inward-moving spiral and an outward-moving spiral. Energy travels in and out along these spiral pathways, passing through three levels, which act like gateways or valves that serve to transmute the energy to the appropriate level. At the innermost centre of the chakra there is a connection to the core of the body, usually into the spinal column. The chakras extend outwards from both the front and back of the physical body and span the levels of the aura, i.e. the subtle bodies that surround our physical body (*see* p.55).

Chakras function like energy transformers. They act as entry points or assimilators; they facilitate the distribution and flow of life force throughout the whole energy system; they are the doorways or access points through which we can give out, release or inadvertently leak energy. Our state of being at all levels, physical, emotional, mental and spiritual, will affect the chakras and their ability to absorb, transmute and give out energy.

Chakras can malfunction in a number of ways. They may seem sluggish and lethargic, unable to respond efficiently to incoming and outgoing energies. Conversely, they may appear overactive, overcharged and seem to be spinning out of control. Sometimes a chakra will feel as if it has been totally over-extended resulting in an over-stretched feeling. This may cause it to appear stuck wide open. Occasionally chakras seem to have a shattered or fragmented appearance. This is often seen in patients who have experienced some sort of trauma or shock. Usually chakras have a circular or cone-like appearance, but it is possible for them to appear pulled out of shape so they may become elliptical. They may also be pushed off centre and out of position.

A balanced and strong chakra system is vital for good health and well-being on all levels. Ideally, all seven will be balanced in relation to each other so energy flows in an even manner throughout the system. However, imbalances can occur when we undergo major shifts in spiritual consciousness and growth, therefore occasional imbalances need not be a cause for concern.

CRYSTALS AND THE CHAKRA SYSTEM

Crystals can support, strengthen and re-structure the chakra system in a number of ways. The most commonly used method is to place carefully chosen crystals directly onto the chakras. The choice of crystals and intention of the therapist will determine the effect on the chakras, which may be to encourage an opening and expansion or closing and contracting of the energy centres. Crystals may assist the chakras to have an increased receptivity to the healing universal life force or to help transport energy more effectively between the physical and spiritual dimensions.

Sometimes all seven chakras are worked upon at the same time with what are commonly known as 'chakra sets'. Usually seven differently coloured crystals matching the rainbow spectrum colours (red, orange, yellow, green, blue, indigo and violet) will be used. Traditionally each chakra is thought to have a corresponding rainbow colour, starting with red for the base chakra, moving up to orange for the sacral chakra etc. Each chakra resonates with the other six. Therefore, any crystal placed on one chakra will also affect all the others. Also, all seven crystals must harmonize and balance with one another, so creating such sets is a complex and skilled task.

However, only rarely do all seven chakras need to be treated, so it can be far more potent to work on just one or two chakras. When these are functioning at an optimum level, the whole system will naturally come back into balance.

If the practitioner wishes to unify the whole chakra system or imbue it with just one vibration, a set of seven identical crystals may be used. This method is less commonly used yet it is far simpler and can be very powerful. Care should be taken that the chakra set consists only of crystals that are equally compatible for all seven chakras. For example, a heavier and solid crystal such as hematite may sit very comfortably on the base chakra but may not be so appropriate for the sensitive brow chakra. It is easier to imagine more general all-purpose crystals such as rose quartz or aventurine being placed equally effectively on the crown and brow chakras or the base and sacral chakras.

In addition to placing crystals directly onto the chakras, patterns of crystal may be placed around the chakras to give support and structure whilst they undergo a shift in consciousness or to help them reform to their correct shape. Alternatively, crystals may be positioned between two chakras to form a 'bridge' or link to help the energy travel more easily between the two energy centres, thereby helping energy to flow unimpeded throughout the system.

51

RIGHT AVENTURINE IS A SUITABLE CRYSTAL TO USE SAFELY ON ALL SEVEN CHAKRAS.

THE SEVEN MAIN CHAKRAS

1. CROWN CHAKRA (*SAHASRARA*) – LOCATED AT A POINT JUST ABOVE THE TOP OF THE HEAD. SOME SYSTEMS BELIEVE THAT ITS POSITION CORRELATES TO THE 'SOFT SPOT' OR FONTANELLE IN THE SKULL. IT IS CONSIDERED TO BE THE PHYSICAL ENTRY AND EXIT POINT FOR SPIRIT.

2. BROW CHAKRA (*AJNA*) – IT IS ALSO CALLED THE THIRD EYE, AND IS GENERALLY LOCATED IN THE MIDDLE OF THE FOREHEAD, ROUGHLY FOLLOWING THE LINE OF THE BRIDGE OF THE NOSE.

3. THROAT CHAKRA (*VISUDDHA*) – LOCATED IN THE NECK, OVER THE LARYNX AND THYROID GLAND.

4. HEART CHAKRA (*ANAHATA*) – POSITIONED AT THE CENTRE OF THE CHEST AREA, ALIGNED WITH THE HEART.

5. SOLAR PLEXUS (*MANIPURA*) – LOCATED IN THE UPPER STOMACH AREA, APPROXIMATELY 10CM BELOW THE TIP OF THE STERNUM.

6. SACRAL CHAKRA (*SVADISTHANA*) – ALSO REFERRED TO AS THE HARA, SOMETIMES THE SPLEEN CHAKRA. IT IS LOCATED APPROXIMATELY 5–10CM BELOW THE NAVEL.

7. BASE CHAKRA (*MULADHARA*) – ALSO CALLED THE ROOT CHAKRA. IT IS LOCATED AT THE BASE OF THE SPINE

52

ABOVE MANY CRYSTAL THERAPISTS WORK WITH THE CHAKRA SYSTEM, CORRECTING ANY IMBALANCES THAT MANIFEST AS PHYSICAL OR EMOTIONAL PROBLEMS.

TRADITIONAL CHAKRA/CRYSTAL CORRESPONDENCES

1. FOR THE CROWN CHAKRA, TRY USING A WHITE OR CLEAR STONE. GOLDEN OR VIOLET STONES SUCH AS AMETHYST MAY ALSO SUIT THIS CHAKRA.

2. IN THE CENTRE OF THE FOREHEAD AT THE BROW CHAKRA, DARK BLUE OR VIOLET STONES ARE TRADITIONALLY USED, SUCH AS LAPIS LAZULI.

3. AT THE THROAT CHAKRA JUST ABOVE THE STERNAL NOTCH, USE LIGHT BLUE STONES SUCH AS BLUE LACE AGATE, TURQUOISE OR AQUAMARINE.

4. A GREEN STONE SUCH AS JADE, AVENTURINE OR MALACHITE MAY BE USED AT THE HEART CHAKRA. A SMALL PINK STONE MAY ALSO BE ADDED.

5. YELLOW OR GOLDEN STONES, SUCH AS CITRINE, TIGER'S EYE, AMBER OR TOPAZ, ARE OFTEN PLACED ON THE SOLAR PLEXUS CHAKRA.

6. THE SACRAL CHAKRA MAY BE BALANCED BY AN ORANGE STONE SUCH AS CARNELIAN, ORANGE CALCITE OR A DARK CITRINE QUARTZ.

7. RED STONES, SUCH AS GARNET OR SPINEL, CAN BE PLACED AT THE BASE CHAKRA, EITHER BETWEEN THE LEGS OR BENEATH THE COCCYX.

8. CONSIDER PLACING A DARK CITRINE, SMOKY QUARTZ, HEMATITE OR BLACK TOURMALINE BY THE FEET TO STABILIZE AND GROUND ALL THE ENERGIES.

ABOVE NOVICE HEALERS MAY USE SEVEN DIFFERENT COLOURED CRYSTALS, KNOWN AS 'CHAKRA SETS', TO CORRESPOND WITH THE ASSOCIATED CHAKRA COLOUR. MORE EXPERIENCED THERAPISTS, HOWEVER, WILL OFTEN CONSIDER THE MORE SUBTLE ASPECTS OF THE CHAKRAS WHEN SELECTING CRYSTAL CHAKRA SETS.

Centres that seem congested or blocked by energetic debris may be cleared. New levels of healing light energy can be pulsed into the chakras. Gifted and well-trained therapists are sometimes able to re-structure or re-build damaged chakras. Discs or slices of crystal may be placed over the energy centre or crystal wands may be used to 're-etch' the shape of the chakra. However, this is highly specialized work and should only be carried out by practitioners who are very experienced.

Quite frequently a pendulum is used to dowse the chakras to assess their state and also to balance them. This method should be used with caution, however. The chakras are very susceptible to any circular movements and it is possible to cause mis-alignment with this method. A safer alternative is to place one hand over the chakra to be dowsed and hold the pendulum well away from the patient and the therapist and then proceed to dowse. Rather than using a simple 'yes/no' system with the pendulum, we prefer to teach our practitioners how to use the pendulum to give a physical demonstration of how the energy is flowing through the chakras. With this method, it is possible to ascertain the outline of the chakras and the levels of energy that are entering and leaving. We check the shape of the chakra, looking mainly for a balanced rounded shape. We also look at the size of the chakra, the aim being that all the chakras are of similar size and neither over extended nor too contracted. Finally, we look at the speed with which the energy travels through the chakras – a balanced even flow is ideal. We would look to redress the balance if there was an erratic flow or if any of the chakras appeared to be spinning either far too fast or too sluggishly.

The practitioner may also 'scan' the chakras with their hand, sensing any imbalances. Some practitioners will draw

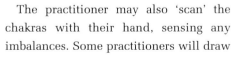

LEFT SOME CRYSTAL THERAPISTS WILL SCAN A PATIENT'S BODY WITH THEIR HANDS TO FIND ANY IMBALANCES IN THE CHAKRAS.

upon their knowledge of the functions of the chakras, and by working through the case history of the patient will deduce which chakras require attention. For example, a persistent sore throat may indicate a blocked throat chakra that needs to be cleared.

In addition to the seven major chakras, there are many more smaller, but no less important, energy centres, which are sometimes referred to as 'minor chakras'. These usually occur at key points in the body where energy lines meet and cross, for example, the palms of the hands, soles of the feet, ears, shoulders, hips and knees are all positions where minor chakras are found.

Crystal therapists will sometimes place crystals on the minor chakras. Usually work on minor chakras will support the healing that is being directed towards one of the major chakras. For example, work on the throat chakra may also involve placing crystals on the shoulder chakra points. Sometimes extremely complex interlocking patterns are formed, these can have a very powerful effect on the patient. Such techniques should only be carried out by skilled therapists who are highly sensitive to the subtle energies involved.

55

The Aura and the Subtle Bodies

Around every physical body there is an energy field that is commonly known as the aura. This field of subtle energy is perceived in various forms by different psychics and healers. Generally, the aura is considered to be made up of several layers or levels commonly referred to as the 'subtle bodies'.

The aura could be likened to an energetic communication system. It helps us to communicate with other levels of consciousness and realms, sometimes quite unconsciously. Our instinctive reactions to people, situations and atmospheres are caused by our aura contracting or expanding. We can absorb impressions and feelings on many subtle levels – these interactions are taking place through the various levels of the aura.

An understanding of the subtle bodies is important for all vibrational healers because healing often takes place within the subtle bodies before it manifests in the physical body. Moreover, the cause of the illness may be located within the aura and not the physical body.

Some teachers view the aura as being made up of separate layers that surround the body, similar to layers in an onion. Others teach that the layers overlay and inter-penetrate one another.

LEFT THE AURA IS AN ENERGY FIELD THAT SURROUNDS THE PHYSICAL BODY. IT IS COMPOSED OF SEVERAL LAYERS, KNOWN AS 'SUBTLE BODIES'.

THE LEVELS OF THE AURA

Some traditions teach that there are four layers in the aura relating to the physical, emotional, mental and spiritual. Other traditions subscribe to the belief that there are seven layers that correspond to the seven chakras.

LEVEL 1: The Etheric Body – this is the densest of all the subtle bodies. It is the layer that is closest to the physical body and corresponds to the base chakra. This is the subtle body that is most usually first seen by novice clairvoyants. Its shape loosely resembles the physical body outline. The etheric body relates to the mineral realm including rocks, metals and crystals as well as the physical body.

LEVEL 2: The Astral Body – also know as the Emotional Body. It corresponds to the sacral chakra. Emotion is experienced at this level and causes of disease due to emotion and trauma are often found in this part of the energy field. This level relates to the plant realm and issues connected with emotions, reactions and thoughts can show up here.

LEVEL 3: The Lower Mental Body – sometimes simply called the Mental Body, corresponds to the solar plexus chakra. Our mental processes register here, as do issues relating to ego. Interestingly heartache often registers here. This level relates to the animal realm – fears, instincts and intuitive responses can show up at this level.

These first three levels are strongly connected to physical and personal being. Often the origins of diseases will have their root cause anchored in one of these bodies, and therefore therapists often find themselves working in one of these first three levels. The next level can be considered a bridge or turning point where the aura starts to reach out to more subtle and spiritual realms.

57

LEVEL 4: The Higher Mental Body – also called by some individuals the Intuitional Body – relates to the heart chakra and is the point where we start relating to the universe and move beyond our own personal realm of awareness. True unconditional love can be expressed in this part of the aura. This layer relates to the human realm and the human condition.

ABOVE A HEALTHY AURA WILL BE COMPOSED OF BRIGHT, EVENLY BALANCED COLOURS.

LEVEL 5: The Intuitional Body – also known as the Spiritual Body or the Causal Body – it relates to the throat chakra and is considered by some teachers to be the interface between physical matter and the spiritual universal consciousness. Through this level of the aura, we are able to travel beyond personal experience and connect to an inter-planetary level of collective consciousness that can make us aware of the small but vital part we play within the greater whole.

LEVEL 6: The Spiritual Body – also known as the Soul Body, the Monadic Body or the Celestial Body. This part of the energy field corresponds to the brow chakra and relates to the expression of higher spiritual consciousness. It takes us into the realm of the angelic. In this part of the aura you may register the presence of Divine guidance and messengers. Here you may also become extremely sensitive to subtle vibrationary influences and aware of a need to increase your energy protection.

LEVEL 7: The Divine Body – also know as the Celestial Body – this correlates to the crown chakra and is the part of the aura that is the heavenly connection to the Divine. Through this level of the aura you can connect with all that is within all dimensions at the highest vibrationary levels – this is the realm of Divine universality.

BECOMING SENSITIVE TO THE AURA

Try a simple exercise to help you to develop your sensitivity to the different layers within the aura. Stand in front of or behind a friend and place the palm of your hand lightly on the side of their upper arm. Now draw your hand slowly away from their arm moving out to their side, until your hand is about two metres away. Then very slowly draw your hand back to the starting point on the side of their upper arm. With practice and careful observation you will be able to detect very slightly different sensations in the palms of your hands. You may feel heat, cold, pressure or tingling at certain times. This is almost certainly occurring when you are passing through different layers of the aura. As you become more experienced you may also feel blockages and congestion within the aura.

The aura is extremely sensitive to all kinds of vibrations and you can test this for yourself. Starting with the exercise described above, find a part of the aura that feels quite buoyant or solid. Now ask your friend to think of someone or something that makes them feel happy. As their aura fills with their positive and happy thoughts you will be able to feel the energy field increase in size and possibly become more buoyant.

59

CRYSTALS AND THE SUBTLE BODIES

Sometimes even experienced therapists fail to realize what a dramatic effect crystals can have on the aura. Working on a vulnerable area in the aura with just a small subtle movement and a carefully tuned crystal can have a tremendous impact on the patient and should be used carefully and cautiously. A small action on only one part of the aura can have a knock-on effect on the whole area and bring about a very deep and powerful experience for the patient. Please bear this important point in mind if you decide to try any of the

The therapist may 'oscillate' a crystal in various parts of the aura. This is especially helpful for loosening debris or negative patterns that may have become lodged in the aura. Usually a smooth crystal is used such as a crystal sphere or egg or possibly a large tumble stone. This is held between the palms of the hands and gently rotated, rocked or oscillated within the aura.

AURA BRUSHING

Aura brushing is a technique that involves brushing a crystal
through the aura to cleanse it of any debris, tease out any congestion
or to help separate the layers within the aura. It is a perfect pick-
me-up after a long, hard day, especially if there have been lots of
negative thoughts around that could have adhered to the aura. It is
also a useful technique to finish off a healing session as the crystal
is combed down towards the ground and can help earth the aura.
The therapist may use a variety of crystals for this, depending on
what is required. A small cluster of amethyst could be used, a
chunk of rose quartz or the side of a quartz point. The point should
not be directed towards the aura as this could be too directional and
'sharp' for the aura. Instead, hold the crystal so the point is directed
towards the palm of your hand or held by a
fingertip and only the side of the crystal is
exposed. The side is then used to brush
through the aura.

RIGHT AMETHYST IS AN IDEAL CRYSTAL
TO USE FOR CLEANSING THE AURA.

Seven crystals, each one carefully selected to work on a different
level of the aura, may be placed beside the patient or below their
feet. The patient, guided by the healer who would channel healing
energy at the same time, would breathe in or absorb the healing
vibrations of the appropriate crystals into each of the levels of
the aura in turn. As in the case of chakra sets, it is important that
these seven crystals harmonize with one another and display a
cohesive theme.

Crystal layouts, which involve crystals being placed around the
body, inevitably affect the subtle bodies. Ideally, the therapist will be

fully aware of which level they are working on when placing the crystals in a particular formation. Also, because the aura usually expands as it relaxes and receives healing, it is important that the therapist adjusts the positions of the crystals placed around the body in accordance with this expansion.

MERIDIANS

The meridian system is integral to many ancient Eastern healing philosophies such as shiatsu, chi kung and acupuncture. The meridians are the pathways along which energy can travel through the body. In Chinese medicine the energy that runs along these pathways is usually referred to as *chi* or *qi*.

There are 14 major meridians. These comprise 12 paired meridians, one on each side of the body. In addition, there are two further meridians that run singly, along the central column of the body – the Central Meridian runs up the front of the body from the pubic bone to the lower lip and the Governor Meridian runs up the back of the body along the spine from the coccyx over the head to the upper lip.

Each of the 12 paired meridians is linked to an organ in the body. It should be borne in mind that the meridian relates to the general function of the organ, not its specific physical location and structure.

Along the meridian pathway lies various key acupuncture/ acupressure points – these points should be used with great caution and only by skilled and knowledgeable therapists as it is easy to cause imbalance and potential problems by interfering with the flow of the meridians.

The meridians flow in one direction only and it is important that therapists be aware of the energy flow direction. Each pair of meridians is either yin (feminine principle) or yang (masculine principle). Yin meridians flow upwards from Earth to Heaven. Yang meridians flow downwards from Heaven to Earth.

61

THE MAIN MERIDIANS

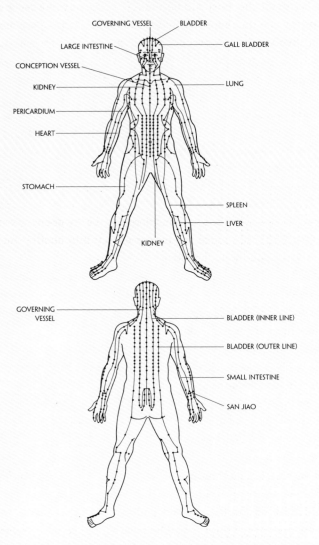

ABOVE THERE ARE 14 MAIN MERIDIANS (OR ENERGY CHANNELS) IN THE BODY, ALONG WHICH *CHI* FLOWS.

CRYSTALS AND MERIDIANS

Crystals can very effectively be applied to the meridian system. In most cases, the therapist will be aiming to clear any blockages so that the energy can flow more easily and freely through the system. This might involve placing crystals at each end of the meridian, placing crystals on strategic points or 'tracing' the meridian with a crystal. Tracing describes the action of drawing a crystal along the meridian pathway, sometimes just touching the skin but more usually a few centimetres above the physical body – it is important that the direction of the meridian is followed. **NB: This is of vital importance when working on the heart meridian.**

If there is excess energy in one meridian, crystals may be used to calm the energy down. The meridians are considered to be linked into a continuous cycle, i.e. one meridian leads into another. Therefore, if a meridian is considered to be 'over-energized', the therapist will often move the excess energy into another meridian that is correspondingly depleted.

63

Crystals can be very effective substitutes for acupuncture needles. The therapist may direct the point of a crystal towards various acupuncture points along the meridian pathway. Frequently, a single terminated crystal such as a clear quartz point, or tourmaline crystals, which often have a wand-like appearance, will be used. Sometimes the therapist will tape small crystals to the various acupuncture points along the meridian. The stimulation or activation of these points will vary according to which crystals are used and on which points.

These are complex and potentially very powerful techniques. They should only be used by skilled and fully trained crystal therapists who have in-depth knowledge of the meridian system and the power of crystals.

ABOVE A CRYSTAL CAN BE TAPED TO AN ACUPUNCTURE POINT ALONG THE MERIDIAN.

THE GRID LINES –
LINES OF THE UNIVERSAL WEB

Many crystal healing techniques involve placing crystals in patterns around the body. These are very commonly patterns of 6, 8 or 12 crystals. The theory underlying these patterns is rarely explained, although the benefits of the patterns are often expounded.

ICCH teaches a system that explains the basic underlying theory of patterns based on the lines of the Universal Web or Weave, also known as the Fabric of Creation. This involves basic sacred geometry and the creation of form. This theory is simply taught under the heading of 'Grid Lines'.

There are three main directions of energy based on the three-fold principle or trinity of active, passive and neutral.

The active or masculine principle relates to a single line of energy that runs vertically through the core of the body – this approximately corresponds to a central line running from the top of the head and along the spine. This active line of energy runs from Heaven to Earth and Earth to Heaven.

There are three passive or feminine 'gateways' that run horizontally across the body. Their positions may vary very slightly from individual to individual. Usually the top gate runs across the upper chest in line with the collar bone just below the throat chakra. The second gate runs along the centre of the torso roughly in line with the waist,

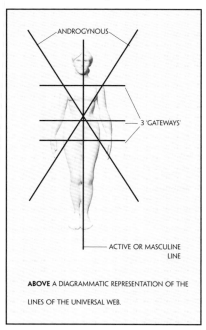

ANDROGYNOUS

3 'GATEWAYS'

ACTIVE OR MASCULINE LINE

ABOVE A DIAGRAMMATIC REPRESENTATION OF THE LINES OF THE UNIVERSAL WEB.

slightly above the navel and below the solar plexus chakra. The third gate runs across the hips and pelvic region, approximately 3–4in below the navel along the top of the pubic bone and below the sacral chakra.

The neutral or androgynous lines run diagonally across the body roughly from shoulder to opposite hip – these vary most between individuals and the cross-over point may intersect just below the heart chakra to almost the centre of the sacral chakra.

If a crystal is placed at each end of all of these lines there will be a total of 12 crystals placed around the body. However, it is more common practice to activate only some of these lines, and therefore patterns may be created consisting of just four, six or eight crystals.

ICCH students are taught to activate these lines in accordance with the needs of the patient. Invariably, the active (masculine) line will be anchored in some way as this acts as a lynchpin for the whole of this aspect of the energetic system. One or more of the feminine gates may also be worked on depending upon the individual's need. Each gate has a specific function (see below). Alternatively, the androgynous lines will be balanced and activated to help bring the patient into greater balance.

The active line governs the flow of life force from Heaven down to Earth and from Earth back to Heaven. It is the conduit or channel through which the universal life force or Divine energy passes. It is via this channel that we are able to bring spiritual energy into the material plane and offer back the physical perspective up to spirit. As already said, the active line will usually be anchored in some way as this line is a vital part of the system upon which the other grid lines are hinged. If this line is perceived as weak within the patient, then crystals with strengthening and reinforcing qualities will be used. If it is perceived as too dominant then softening or muting crystals may be used. However, the general aim is to bring weaker parts of the grid up to strength rather than reducing the strength of existing lines.

The three gates are based on the principle that is seen elsewhere in the subtle energy system, namely the chakras, which have a similar valve or gateway system to help step up and down the universal life flow. In simple and everyday terms, these gates or valves allow the powerful celestial energy to be fed into the energy system in digestible doses. Without these gates there is a risk of overdosing on too much spiritual energy or life force.

The first gate, which runs across the shoulders, might be entitled 'the gateway of initiation'. It is here that the individual chooses whether to accept the incoming spiritual frequencies or not. Often this decision accompanies some major life changes or challenges, which could be described as a form of initiation.

The second gate, which is located horizontally at waist level, could be entitled 'the gateway of balance'. At this point the spiritual energy integrates more fully into the life of the individual. Tests involving the ego could occur now, more personal responsibility is required in order for this spiritual energy to be used wisely and with love. Balance is needed and a conscious choice regarding how to use the new spiritual frequencies.

The third gate, which we normally call 'the gateway of manifestation', is located at hip level. The spiritual energy has been accepted, a choice has been made to work with it positively and now, for some, the greatest test of all is to earth it. Spiritual energy has to be made manifest. To bring spirit into matter is possibly the ultimate spiritual challenge. This gate is often found to malfunction, so many people become wonderfully inspired (first gate), have amazing ideas and plans for that inspiration (second gate) but sadly, due to a closed third gate, the plans and ideas fail to materialize.

The androgynous or neutral lines are the two diagonal lines running across the body from the shoulder to the opposite hip. Their position and angles of separation vary greatly. It should be noted that the crossover point can be as high up on the torso as the heart chakra level or low down at almost the sacral chakra level. This crossover point carries a lot of energy and is sometimes mistaken for a chakra.

In some individuals it is almost impossible to perceive the presence of the androgynous grid lines. In these circumstances, it is usually necessary to work on the active and passive grid lines in the first instance, bringing these to a degree of balance and harmony. When this has been achieved, the androgynous grid lines may then start to show up. The main theme of these lines is integration and balance. As the spiritual frequencies flow through the system, there has to be a compatible mix of action and receptivity. To allow this to occur, a point of stillness and neutrality is also required. When these lines are strongly aligned within us, we can simply 'be with spirit'.

CRYSTALS AND THE GRID LINES

A sensitive and gifted crystal therapist is able to gently support the grid system to help the patient fulfil his or her potential. It is important that the grid is appropriately balanced and strengthened as needed, but not artificially reinforced with crystals, nor over-energized. If too much energy is placed into a grid line it will not be able to sustain the new level of activity when the crystals are removed, unless there is a continued supply of crystal energy. This is obviously not a practical proposition, nor is it helpful in the long term!

It is important to recognize the individual needs of each energy line and support it with the appropriate matched pairing of crystals. Usually complementary pairs of crystals are used, so the crystals can form a two-way channel of communication that become an almost physically tangible energy line.

The practitioner aims to ensure that there is a clear two-way flow of energy through all the lines (this is especially important with the active line), and that each line is strongly structured and present within the energy system.

Also, each line should be in its optimum position. This will usually be achieved by placing pairs of crystals, one on each end of the grid line. In this way, patterns of crystals will be created that will also form various geometric shapes, which will bring their own power to the healing.

For example, if the active line is anchored as well as the two androgynous lines, then a total of six crystals will be used, giving a six-pointed star pattern that is often referred to as the Star of David. This is also thought to symbolize the coming together of spirit and matter by way of the two interlocking triangles. This is an especially appropriate pattern considering that the main aim of such a layout would be to help the Heaven-Earth flow and ensure that it comes through with balance and harmony.

LEFT THE STAR OF DAVID SYMBOLIZES THE COMING TOGETHER OF SPIRIT AND MATTER.

Occasionally more than two crystals will be used on a grid line. For example, a pair of quartz points will be placed facing towards each other to create a clearing and strengthening line of energy. However, the therapist may consider this to be too powerful or feel that an additional frequency is also required. Two rose quartz tumble stones might be added just inside each of the quartz points to act as a filter and to ensure that their vibration is also added to the grid line. Also, crystals may be substituted during the session to enhance the opening of a gateway, to support a grid line or slow the energy that is travelling through one part of the pattern.

A few therapists are able to activate the grid lines using a crystal tool such as a wand or energy channelled from their hands. This is extremely skilled work and should only be carried out by very experienced therapists who have specialized in this type of work.

WORKING WITH CRYSTALS

CHAPTER FIVE

CHOOSING CRYSTALS

Choosing a crystal is one of the most important aspects of working with crystals. Whether you wish to go out and buy a new crystal or are selecting one with a special task in mind from your personal collection, follow the guidelines set out below.

There is a wealth of books, leaflets and charts detailing what crystals are supposed to 'do'. However, these are all based on the experiences of the people who wrote them and they frequently contradict each other. We believe that every person is intuitively aware of their own healing needs. Therefore, we would urge you to ignore other people's recommendations and compile your own reference list of

LEFT CHOOSING A CRYSTAL IS A PERSONAL MATTER. LISTEN TO YOUR INTUITION.

what is true and right for you at this time. Different people will have a different experience from the same crystal and two crystals of the same type will affect the same person differently. In other words, we do not feel that it is possible to simply list the properties of crystals and say that all amethyst crystals are good for one thing and all clear quartz crystals are good for another. If you work with two very similar looking pieces of amethyst you will almost certainly find differences between them.

FOCUS ON THE PURPOSE

Whenever choosing a crystal, keep your thoughts focused very clearly on the purpose you have in mind for the crystal.

Have a few moments of silence, clear your mind of all thoughts. Within the stillness, begin to build a clear image of what you would like the crystal to do to assist you.

If, for example, you are looking for a crystal to help in your meditation work, then hold that thought clearly in your mind. Imagine that your entire being is attuned to discovering a crystal specifically to aid you in your meditation practice.

REMAIN WELL EARTHED

Maintaining your connection to the planet will help you more clearly and easily recognize your crystal. You are also less likely to be distracted by all the other crystals vying for your attention, and are therefore less likely to become dizzy or light headed (*see* p.79 for more on earthing).

BE RECEPTIVE

While keeping your thoughts focused, notice which crystal calls you. You may like the look of it or feel very attracted to it. You may instinctively want to pick it up. Allow yourself to be attracted to certain crystals without feeling the need to justify your decision. Remember anyone can choose a crystal because it looks nice, you, however, are allowing energy to follow thought!

TIPS TO HELP YOU CHOOSE A CRYSTAL

Whilst focused, earthed and receptive, apply some or all of the following methods:-

1. LOOKING

As you glance at a collection of crystals, one may catch your eye and draw your attention to it. Maybe it is not the largest, clearest or most beautiful crystal – in fact it might appear quite ordinary or boring, nestling in the corner of the shelf, or basking in the shadow of a slightly grander, more extravagant example. Do not be put off by these first impressions, learn to recognize the crystal that first called you and most importantly of all trust your intuition.

2. ENERGY SCANNING

This is a technique that is best practised in an environment that is sympathetic to energy workers, such as a New Age shop. Using whichever hand feels most comfortable to you, place your hand parallel to the table, palm down and slowly pass your hand over the selection of crystals. You may feel an intensification of energy, heat, tingling or even some form of mild electric shock as complementary energies meet.

Be aware of moving the hand slowly and be prepared to go over a particular area more than once. The brain may register the 'signal' just after your hand has passed over the crystal, so you may need to backtrack. If the crystals are particularly close together, it may be helpful to isolate a few that you have received a feeling from, spread them out, then try again to locate the optimum one.

ABOVE IF PRACTICAL, YOU MAY LIKE TO SCAN A SELECTION OF CRYSTALS BEFORE CHOOSING THE ONE YOU WISH TO BUY.

71

3. 'IT FEELS RIGHT'

Choose a crystal that appears to attract you, and take hold of the crystal in your hands. Does it feel comfortable? Does it look as though it belongs there? Does it feel right? Do you have no idea why you are attracted, although there is no denying that you are? If the answer is yes then this is the right crystal. Trust that feeling.

ABOVE IF A CRYSTAL FEELS RIGHT WHEN YOU HOLD IT, THEN IT IS PROBABLY THE RIGHT CHOICE FOR YOU.

CLEANSING CRYSTALS

There are many reasons why we cleanse crystals. When they first find their way to us they will have been handled by various people, some of whom may not have been in a positive frame of mind. Also consider the trauma of the mining process, which could include the use of violent explosives and cleaning with strong chemicals. Crystals are very sensitive to thought vibrations and it is therefore possible that some negative energy may have been absorbed.

Cleansing a crystal, when you first become its 'custodian', is part of a ritual that helps you to get to know one another. As you carry out the cleansing process, your energies merge and your vibrations start to tune in to one another. Most healers agree that it is important to cleanse their 'working' crystals after each patient. If you use your crystals for healing other people, they may feel sticky or lose their shine as they absorb negativity. The frequency and type of cleansing depends on what the crystal has encountered in terms of energy – a hard working healing crystal will usually need more frequent cleansing than one that stays at home to help with your dreams.

How to Cleanse Your Crystals

Various ways of cleansing crystals include:-

1. Soaking in salt water solution – approximately 1 pint of water to one teaspoon of rock salt. The length of time the crystal is left in the solution depends on the needs of the crystal and the type of crystal. Other ingredients can be added to this mixture such as: cider vinegar, Bach Flower Remedies (particularly Rescue Remedy) or cleansing aromatherapy oils i.e. grapefruit or rosemary.

LEFT SOAK YOUR CRYSTAL IN A SALT WATER SOLUTION TO GET RID OF ANY NEGATIVE ENERGY.

2. Holding under running water – a stream, waterfall, water from the tap or even in the waves of the sea. Natural sources are preferred although city healers do have to be practical!

RIGHT RUNNING WATER CAN BE USED TO CLEANSE YOUR CRYSTALS. THIS WILL HELP TO RESTORE ITS NATURAL BALANCE.

3. Bury in the earth or some sand.

4. Place in sunlight and or moonlight for several days, either outdoors or on a windowsill.

5. Use visualization, imagine that pure brilliant light is streaming through and 'washing' the crystal.

6. Smudging with herbs (i.e. passing the crystals through the smoke of a small bunch of burning herbs or incense).

7. Using sound either by chanting, placing within a Tibetan singing bowl or directing sound waves from a different source through the crystal.

There are some practical considerations to remember. The water temperature should never be extreme. Some crystals such as celestite are very soft and fragile and so suit methods such as smudging rather than immersion in water. Halite is a salt crystal and will dissolve in a water solution. Metallic crystals such as iron pyrites and hematite can be washed briefly in water, but it is preferable not to soak them for a long time as they may become a little tarnished.

There are no set rules as to when a crystal needs cleansing. As you become more familiar with your crystals, you will develop a sense of when it is necessary. Some professional healers, who work with several patients in one day, cleanse their crystals between each healing session using a swift visualization method. Others prefer to have several crystals and use different stones on different patients. They then cleanse all the crystals at the end of each day. It is a matter of personal preference and each healer must find his or her own way.

DEDICATING CRYSTALS

Dedicating crystals ensures that they can only be used for good and acts as a safeguard that protects anyone, including yourself, who works with the crystal. Whenever we acquire a new crystal we carry out a brief and simple ritual. This involves visualizing light streaming from the Divine source through the crystal. At the same time we ask that the crystal may only be used in a good and positive way. This is to ensure the crystal is lovingly used for light-filled purposes.

A DEDICATION

To dedicate your crystal either speak out loud or silently think about how you wish the crystal to work. It is preferable to choose your own words and image but you may like to use the following:

'From this point on may this crystal only be used in the name of love and light and always for good and higher purpose. May only the purest, highest and finest energies be channelled through this crystal and may it work always in accordance with Divine Will.'

KEEPING YOUR CRYSTALS SAFE

Crystals vary in hardness. Softer crystals, for example celestite and fluorite, will be damaged if rubbed harshly against harder minerals such as topaz, ruby, sapphire and diamond. Minerals of the same hardness can also cause damage to one another. It is therefore advisable to keep each crystal in its own separate container or pouch. If you like to carry your crystals around with you, consider using a sectioned-off jewellery box or roll. Crystals are also well protected if wrapped in ordinary newspaper.

Be aware of the amount of dust that crystals may collect when kept on shelves, particularly on softer crystals such as celestite and fluorite as the dust particles may be harder and can damage the surface lustre of the crystal, causing a dulled or pitted exterior appearance. A covered cabinet may be a convenient solution.

You may like to keep your crystals regularly 'nourished' by regularly exposing them to sunlight and moonlight. There is no problem with this providing that you are aware of the problems of dust with softer minerals. Note, however, that some minerals will fade or change colour after long exposure to sunlight.

RIGHT PLACE YOUR CRYSTALS IN A
COMPARTMENTALIZED BOX TO KEEP
THEM SAFE AND FREE FROM DUST.

POISONOUS AND DANGEROUS CRYSTALS

As a general precaution, always wash your hands after handling crystals or minerals. As a part of the mining process, the crystals may have been subjected to acid bath washes as well as other chemical processes and residues of these potentially toxic chemicals could be left on the surface of the crystals. This is also a good reason not to suck or lick crystals, although you may see this being done by some dealers in order to dampen the surface of the mineral and show up its colour. Occasionally some healers like to 'taste' their crystals.

Most crystals are safe to hold. The main exceptions are realgar, a vibrantly bright red mineral containing arsenic, which is relatively easy to obtain, and cinnabar (a mercury-based mineral), which is much rarer. Other poisonous and dangerous minerals exist, including those that are radio-active, but they are not commonly available.

Special care should be taken with a few other minerals. Malachite in its rough unpolished form has small surface dust particles that can cause irritation of the lungs, skin and eyes. You should especially avoid being in a workshop where malachite is being carved or polished, unless wearing suitable protective clothing. Bismuth, which is brightly multi-coloured can cause upset stomachs. It is often very accessible and children find it especially attractive. It should not be put in the mouth. Hands should be washed after handling, and especially before going on to handle food!

Many crystal healing books recommend making crystal or gem elixirs (*see* p.40). However, it is NOT SAFE to do this with many commonly available crystals. Please do not make crystal elixirs for yourself or others until you have received the appropriate training and understand the important safeguards. It is particularly important to avoid using minerals that contain copper, lead, sulphur, mercury, uranium and arsenic. These include turquoise, malachite, some garnets, some tourmalines, sulphur, cinnabar and realgar. Also avoid immersing very soft and crumbly crystals in water.

HEALING WITH CRYSTALS

In order for you to experience for yourself the healing properties of crystals we have outlined below a simple but effective step-by-step procedure to follow. This will ensure that you work safely with your crystals and gain maximum benefit from them.

BEFORE YOU START THE HEALING

First of all cleanse and prepare the space in which you intend to carry out your healing work. You could play some soothing music or burn some incense or aromatherapy oils to freshen up and energetically cleanse the room. This also helps to create a healing atmosphere.

LEFT CREATE THE RIGHT ATMOSPHERE FOR YOUR HEALING WORK BY
LIGHTING A CANDLE. THIS WILL HELP TO PURIFY YOUR SURROUNDINGS.

We recommend you always have a candle burning. It symbolizes the light frequency, which you are aspiring to work with, and helps to purify the atmosphere.

Try to ensure that you will not be interrupted. Allow sufficient time. We suggest that you set aside at least 30 minutes at first, until you become familiar with the process. Later on, as you become more experienced, you may be able to give yourself a 'quickie' five minute healing session, as and when you need it.

Make sure that you have your crystals to hand all in one place so you can make a selection once you have 'attuned' (*see* p.80). We would recommend that all your crystals be 'dedicated' and 'cleansed' beforehand. However, some people like to do this just before they start their healing with the crystal. This is simply a question of personal choice.

RELAXATION

Relaxation enhances the healing process because it helps you to be more receptive to the higher healing frequencies and you will be able to channel light more readily.

Experiment with different relaxation techniques to find what works for you. Try tensing and relaxing various muscle groups of the body or simply stretch and then let the body relax and become softer. Pay attention to your breathing. Take several long slow breaths; imagine that each time you inhale you are absorbing peace and love, and each time you exhale you are releasing feelings of anxiety and tension.

Alternatively, try visualization. Imagine that you are in a tranquil and restful setting. As you create the picture in your mind, your body can relax. Other people find that listening to music can be soothing and relaxing.

EARTHING

Earthing, also sometimes known as 'grounding' refers to the process of anchoring the human energy field to the Earth. Many human beings are unearthed, which means they can feel slightly off-balance, dizzy or disorientated a lot of the time. It is also possible to become unearthed, especially when involved with powerful vibrational healing tools such as crystals. We strongly emphasize earthing in our training programmes.

79

The major benefits of earthing are:

1 You will be able to work towards bringing spirit into matter – this is considered the ultimate spiritual challenge. An evolved spiritual being will be fully present on Earth and carry the spiritual vibration within their being while on Earth in physical form.

2 With a strong Earth link, you can aspire to higher light vibrations and develop a greater capacity to hold the spiritual frequency. In others words, you can be of earthly use as you play your part in the Great Plan.

3 You will gain far more from all your healing work with crystals and any other vibrational healing modalities.

There are various earthing techniques that you can try. Certain crystals (which one depends on you, it varies from individual to individual!) have strong earthing abilities – try holding one or two. Some healers like to place a couple in their socks or wear one on a pendant that they can hold if they feel they are becoming unearthed.

Earthing activities can include mundane household chores, gardening or walking barefoot on some grass or a beach. It is especially helpful to focus on your physical body, especially your feet.

When working with crystals, try to have the soles of your feet flat on the ground. Use visualization to imagine that you have roots growing out of the soles of your feet and from the base of your spine. These roots then extend down into the planet like a solid old oak tree, and you become rooted into the Earth.

Ideally, when you are well earthed, you will feel solid, possibly a little heavier than usual, very clear headed, alert and absolutely focused. Being totally earthed is an asset in daily life as well!

ATTUNEMENT

'Attunement' refers to the process that facilitates an alignment and connection to the inspirational life force, which is fundamental to all creation – we variously refer to this as Light, Great Spirit, Universal Love Energy or God.

There are several stages involved in the attunement process, ensure first that you are relaxed and well earthed, then:

• centre
• protect
• link
• channel

To centre, imagine that you are sitting within a circle or egg shape and you are at the central point of this shape. Alternatively, focus on a point that you feel is at the centre of your being.

Now affirm that only the highest and finest of light frequencies may enter and leave your space. You are protecting your energy field by clearly sending out a thought or intent. You may at this stage want to say a prayer or sacred invocation that is appropriate for you. It is important, however, that you are clear that only the highest light energy that you can carry and that is appropriate for you will enter your space. You may additionally imagine that a shield or coat of light is encompassing you completely. This acts as a protective filter. Also ask that only the high pure and fine vibrations will leave your space. This ensures that the environment is not polluted with any negativity that is released during the healing.

To link to the Light, focus on a feeling of great love and peace. You may wish to visualize that light is pouring down from the sun or a distant star. This Light represents the Divine vibration that you are connecting with and aligning to in order to carry out a healing. Allow yourself to become filled with the Light and allow it to pass through you via your connection into the Earth. For a few moments, become a cosmic doorway through which the Spiritual Vibration may enter into the planet. Allowing the Light to pass all the way through you in this way will help maintain your Earth connection, strengthen your link and ensure that you are aligned to the Light.

81

Once you feel that you are filled with this light, you can start to radiate it outwards from all parts of your being. As you 'channel' the Light, start to direct it towards your crystals as you hold them on your body or place them around you for your healing. As the Light connects with the crystals you may find that they become warmer to hold, lighter or heavier or possibly look different.

The above attunement process ensures that you will be able to receive Divine Guidance as you carry out your healing work with crystals.

SELF-HEALING TECHNIQUES WITH CRYSTALS

TECHNIQUE 1: TO CLEAR, CLEANSE AND ENERGIZE

You will need two single terminated quartz crystals, roughly the same size and shape, which feel compatible with each other.

Method: Hold one quartz point with the point directed away from your body and towards your finger tips and in the other hand hold the other crystal with the point directed towards your arm and your wrist. It does not matter which hand is holding which crystal, but it is important that they feel comfortable. Try holding the crystals in each hand and in different directions to see what feels right for you. Hold in this position for as long as feels comfortable – usually no more than 15 minutes.

This technique is very helpful for clearing and energizing the whole body. It will bring in a new line of energy, almost like a transfusion of crystalline energy. It will also actively draw out and clear any negativity. You may consider using such a technique if there is a 'blockage' such as sinuses, cold or flu, fluid retention, or if you are feeling emotionally 'bunged up'.

VARIATION 1

Choose the crystals as for technique 1.

Instead of placing the crystals in your hands, place the crystals under each foot. One crystal points towards the toes and the other towards the heel. Your feet are flat on the floor with the crystals beneath them. Sit in this position for up to 15 minutes.

The effect is similar to technique 1, but the emphasis is more on discharging and releasing energy blockages. It is very helpful for people who do not release easily through their Earth connection.

VARIATION 2

Choose four clear points instead of two, all roughly the same size and shape. Aim for all four to be compatible with one another.

Hold one crystal in each hand and have one crystal placed under each foot as described in technique 1 and variation 1 above.

This is a combination of the two techniques and is highly energizing and potentially very powerful. It can be very intensive and dynamic; therefore, keep the crystals in position for a maximum of 10 minutes. This technique should be used with extreme caution and only when you feel the need to energize and disperse any blockages. You may find halfway through the healing that you wish to dispense with some of the crystals, either the ones under your feet or those in your hands.

TECHNIQUE 2: TO IMBUE ONE FREQUENCY THROUGHOUT THE ENERGY SYSTEM

You will need one crystal that you have carefully chosen to help you with the self-healing you need at this time.

Method: Place the crystal on a table or on the floor in front of you, in the position where your eyes can easily rest and gaze upon it. At the beginning of the process, imagine that you are drawing light and a healing frequency from the crystal. If you wish, visualize the crystal becoming larger and you becoming smaller until you are totally encompassed in its healing energy. You might even want to imagine that you are able to step into the crystal. At times during the healing you may find it helpful to open your eyes and gaze at the crystal. This can help you maintain your focus.

ABOVE AS YOU LOOK AT THE CRYSTAL, IMAGINE IT BECOMING BIGGER AND BIGGER UNTIL YOU ARE ENCOMPASSED WITHIN ITS HEALING LIGHT.

83

N.B. With this technique, the choosing of the crystal is vitally important because it can be a very powerful technique. You are allowing the crystal frequency to be imbued into your whole energy system from the physical to most subtle levels. This can be very calming and centring, and may be very useful if you feel you need a soothing type of healing, during times of stress or trauma when you need to feel safe and protected.

TECHNIQUE 3: TO WORK ON
SPECIFIC PARTS OF THE BODY

You need one crystal you feel comfortable holding in your hand.

Method: Hold the crystal in one or both hands. Imagine you are absorbing the healing vibration through your hand and that frequency is travelling through your body to the point where it is needed. Vary this technique by holding the crystal on or above the points of the body you wish to work on, even tape or bandage it to an injured part of the body.

This is a localized way of healing, useful for working on specific parts of the body. It is comforting as you can feel the physical presence of the crystal that may actually change texture, temperature and weight; i.e. it can become heavier or lighter during the healing process, in a way that is disproportionate to its physical size.

TECHNIQUE 4: DRAWING OFF BLOCKAGES AND
REDUNDANT PATTERNS IN THE ENERGY FIELD

You need two crystals: one single terminated crystal (i.e. a crystal with a point at one end) and one crystal that feels to you absorbing, passive and receptive, such as a piece of rose quartz, malachite, aventurine or hematite.

Method: Similar to technique 1. Hold the absorbent crystal in one hand and the terminated crystal with the point directed towards your waist in the other hand. Check that you are holding the passive crystal in the hand that is right for you and the active crystal in the other hand. Try both combinations, the crystals should feel balanced with each other and comfortable for you to hold in this way.

During the healing process, visualize a very strong active line of light that travels from the terminated crystal through your body. It clears energy blockages and any redundant patterns that it is time for you to let go of. At the same time, imagine that the passive crystal, which you are holding in the other hand, is drawing the old negative vibrations from your body, holding them, and absorbing these blockages and patterns for you.

OTHER FORMS OF SELF-HEALING

You may wish to utilize an 'ongoing' form of crystal healing such as bandaging or taping a crystal to an area of your body that needs healing. This is known to be extremely effective with injuries such as torn ligaments in knees, tennis elbow etc. In these cases, a small crystal can be slipped into an elasticated bandage or taped to the appropriate area. Similarly, you may wish to wear a crystal that has been tuned and dedicated for a particular type of healing for you.

Another self-healing technique is to work on a photograph of yourself. In this instance, place crystals on or around a photograph of you. Although this seems a simple method, it is surprisingly powerful. Start off with just a few crystals.

At some point during this healing, if you feel strongly that you should put down the absorbent crystal, then do. Follow your intuition. Place the crystal as far away from you as you can without altering your physical position. Then just place your hand palm down towards the Earth and imagine that anything that is being cleared and dispersed is radiating from your hand into the Earth beneath you.

During this technique, you are using a mixture of passive and active energies. One crystal activates and clears energies, whereas the other draws off energies. It can be a very powerful combination, although it may feel deceptively soft and soothing. For this reason, you should not use this technique for very long. This technique is especially useful for people who wish to clear patterns of disease that have been held in the body for a long time.

WHEN NOT TO USE CRYSTALS FOR HEALING

With serious life-threatening conditions we recommend the healer
be well trained and have access to expert support and, if necessary,
supervision from a training college or group of experienced healers.
Extreme caution and care should be taken with the choice of
crystals and techniques in the following cases:

Heart conditions – some experts feel that crystals can over-
stimulate the energy system and special care should be taken
with patients who have a pacemaker. We recommend NOT
placing crystals on the body or near the heart areas and avoid
stimulating crystals.

Pregnancy – you will be dealing with two energy systems,
chakras, auras etc. Frequently the mother-to-be is highly sensitized.
You also need to consider the energy system of the incoming soul.

Epilepsy – some therapists feel that the powerful electrical
impulses of some crystals can be over-stimulating for epileptics and
therefore crystal therapy should not be recommended. However,
this is not something we have personally experienced.

IMPORTANT NOTE: We recommend that crystal therapy
always be utilized holistically. This means that the patient is treated
on many levels – the whole being is healed, not the
disease nor the symptoms.

OTHER WAYS OF WORKING WITH CRYSTALS

CHAPTER SIX

There are limitless possibilities to the beneficial part that crystals can play in our everyday lives. As we explore different ways of working with crystals, we also gain a deeper understanding of how to communicate with them and find further ideas of how to utilize their special gifts.

CRYSTALS AT WORK

COMPUTERS AND VDU SCREENS

VDU and computer screens are thought to cause harm or possible discomfort to the human energy field because of the radiation they emit. A popular antidote is to place a crystal near the screen to diffuse, redirect or counteract these harmful effects. A simple approach is to place a crystal on the top of the VDU or perhaps tape a crystal in an appropriate place on the screen. Alternatively, have a piece of rose

RIGHT ANY HARMFUL VDU ENERGY MAY BE NEGATED BY PLACING A CRYSTAL BETWEEN THE COMPUTER SCREEN AND THE OPERATOR.

quartz strategically placed between the operator and the front of the screen, with the intent that any negativity from the computer be absorbed, transmuted and neutralized.

FOCUS POINTS FOR MEETINGS

There are some quite eminent business people who use spectacular crystals placed in the centre of the table at boardroom and management meetings. The crystals are attuned to help keep the participants inspired, focused and harmonious, therefore working more effectively.

CRYSTALS IN THE HOME

ELECTRICAL EQUIPMENT

Consider placing crystals on or near television screens, microwaves and various other types of electrical equipment in order to transmute any negative vibrations. Home computers, electric radio alarm clocks, cordless telephones and baby listening devices are all considered to be possible sources of electro-magnetic radiation.

CRYSTALS AS ATMOSPHERE ENHANCERS

A properly cleansed, dedicated and attuned crystal can make a very real difference to an individual room as well as an entire house. They are also lovely decorative ornaments.

IN THE KITCHEN

Keep your food fresher for longer by placing crystal in or around foods with a short shelf-life.

Improve the taste of your cake, dough or even casserole mix before you bake it. Place a crystal near (not in) the mixture.

ABOVE CRYSTALS ARE IDEAL FOR THE KITCHEN. THEY WILL HELP TO KEEP FOOD FRESH AND REDUCE UNPLEASANT SMELLS.

This is great for the annual Christmas cake – before putting it in the oven, give it a little extra crystalline ingredient by channelling some energy and loving festive thoughts into the cake mix.

Place a crystal inside or on top of the fridge. Alternatively, make an attractive fridge magnet to place on the front. This will not only keep the food fresher, longer and tasting better but also reduces any bad odours.

Energize your water by having a crystal in or near your water filter or placing a suitably tuned (non-toxic) crystal in a jug of water that is kept in the fridge. It is worth trying to just taste the difference.

CRYSTALS WITH PLANTS AND FLOWERS

AILING PLANTS

Energize the water you use on your plants to revive them and release their full and beautiful potential. To do this, channel healing and loving thoughts into the watering can or jug or place a crystal in the water for a few minutes prior to watering your plants.

Alternatively, place a crystal on the earth of a pot plant that is not thriving. If you feel the roots are weak, try placing a crystal pointing down, directing healing energy towards the roots of the plant. If you want the plant to grow and flourish, try positioning the crystal pointing upwards. Wedge it in the earth around the pot to encourage the direction of energy towards the sky to help the plant grow upwards, tall and strong. Simply placing a crystal near the pot of a plant can often make growth stronger, or keep it growing strongly and fruitfully.

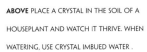

ABOVE PLACE A CRYSTAL IN THE SOIL OF A HOUSEPLANT AND WATCH IT THRIVE. WHEN WATERING, USE CRYSTAL IMBUED WATER .

CUT FLOWERS

Place a group of tumble stones or crystals into the bottom of a vase, then place your flowers into this vase. Not only do the tumble stones or crystals act like a natural oasis and look very attractive in a clear glass vase, but the cut flowers last much longer.

CRYSTAL PEST CONTROL

Make your own insecticide by energizing some water with an appropriately tuned crystal and spray your plants to discourage pests and disease. Be quite specific in your intention otherwise be warned, you may encourage the green fly or other pests to flourish!

FLOWERING TREES AND FRUITS

Use suitably tuned crystals at the root of your apple or fruit trees to encourage an abundance of flowers or fruit and improve the taste and quality of it as well.

VEGETABLE PLOTS

Try planting your vegetables with crystals strategically positioned to promote more prolific growth and better tasting produce. Crystals can also be attuned to ward off slugs and snails to ensure that they do not benefit from all your hard work.

CRYSTALS AND ANIMALS

CAUTION

Animals are very sensitive to crystalline energy and it is very important that you act sensitively and with great responsibility on their behalf. Take extra care when choosing their crystals, which should always be tuned to the highest good for your pet.

Some animals genuinely enjoy having crystals around them. They may take them into their bed or just like to have them close by. Obviously ensure that they avoid chewing rocks and crystals, which could result in harming themselves or the crystals.

A PERSONAL CRYSTAL FOR YOUR PET

You can attach a small crystal pendant or tumble stone to the collar of your cat or dog. The crystal may even be sewn into the collar. A crystal may be suitably dedicated and tuned to keeping them safe or perhaps making sure that they find their way home safely. Do take care to use an appropriately sized crystal so your pet will not be harmed or restricted in any way. A very tiny crystal can be as effective as a larger one. However, monitor that your pet is happy with the crystal because some pets will not like to have a crystal permanently in their energy field.

CRYSTALS AND YOUR PET'S FOOD AND DRINK

Keep a crystal next to your pet's food and water bowls to ensure that they absorb a loving, healing and nourishing vibration or whatever you feel is most appropriate. You might even wish to place an appropriate crystal in the drinking bowl. Take care that the crystal cannot be swallowed or chewed up by an over-eager pet! Make absolutely certain that only non-toxic crystals are used.

ANIMAL BEHAVIOUR

If you have a rather aggressive or assertive animal, keep a crystal by their bed or by their drinking and feeding bowls with the intent that the crystals calm them down and soften their more abrasive personality traits.

CRYSTALS FOR FISH

Fish in aquariums or fish tanks can often benefit from the introduction of carefully chosen crystals. Ensure that the crystal will not leak any poisonous substance when immersed in water –

particularly avoid copper-based minerals such as malachite and turquoise. Also avoid clusters of crystals with sharp points that may harm your fish. Remember that some crystals may have been dipped in acid or other potentially poisonous solutions in order to improve their appearance and market value. Obviously, these should not be used. Crystals in aquariums have been known to keep fish livelier, happier and, as an added bonus, the water cleaner for longer.

USING CRYSTALS AS A STUDY AID

MEMORY AID

If you need to memorize something, perhaps for an exam, try holding a crystal and tuning it to help you memorize and record the information. When you want to remember or recall the information, hold the crystal and re-access it. It may take some practice, but it really does work.

STUDY TIP

Take a crystal, and with the point directed towards the text that you are studying, slowly run the crystal down the side of the page with the crystal tuned so that it will highlight the parts of the text that are most important. As you pass by a sentence or a few words that are particularly relevant to you, it is as if the crystal lights up those words or hesitates slightly. In this way, you can read huge and complex tomes without having to read every word.

A variation on this technique is to take a crystal and 'scan' the text. As you scan the book, intend that the crystal absorbs the information. Then place the crystal under your pillow and ask that as you sleep the crystal imparts the information to you. This can be a very quick and immediate way of learning.

GIFTS

Crystals make marvellous gifts – wedding, Christmas, birthday, anniversary or 'thank you' presents. Not only are they beautiful to look at, but you can, of course, tune them so that they bring harmony, balance and peace into somebody's life.

LEFT SURPRISE AND DELIGHT YOUR FAMILY AND FRIENDS WITH THE GIFT OF A BEAUTIFUL CRYSTAL.

BEAUTY CARE

93

SKINCARE

Make your own rosewater skin tonic by imbuing natural spring water with some rose quartz or similar mineral. Use the tonic daily. After a short time, you will notice a marked improvement in your skin – see how it glows.

Or why not also try making a special crystalline rinse for your hair to give it that extra sheen and body?

ENERGIZING YOUR BEAUTY PRODUCTS AND COSMETICS

Keep a small crystal next to your face creams and make-up. This will ensure that your beauty products work much more effectively, and with minimal application.

TIRED EYES

Use two smooth tumble stones to place over your eyes to soothe puffy, tired eyes. This is a sort of crystalline version of the cucumber slice beauty treatment.

CRYSTALS COMBINED
WITH OTHER THERAPIES

CAUTION

The introduction of crystals into your practice and combining with your own therapy should be carried out with caution. Crystals may make your patients much more sensitive to energetic input. Crystals may also accelerate the healing process so that a patient may experience a deeper sense of relaxation and a deeper aspect of the healing vibration that may lead to a swifter and deeper release of their negativity or past trauma during the treatment. As a therapist working in this way, it is especially important to maintain a clear and energetically pure space working with an awareness that you too will be projecting a more concentrated level of energy.

94

CRYSTALS IN THE HEALING SPACE

Regardless of the therapy being practised, crystals in the waiting room or reception area can bring about a sense of peace and harmony conducive to a healing practice. The crystals can be attuned to radiate loving and positive vibrations, ensuring that a balanced and healthy atmosphere is maintained.

CRYSTALS AND THE THERAPIST

As a therapist, you may also find that it is useful to have a personal crystal in your pocket or worn as jewellery. This can help to keep you personally balanced and centred in order for you to be at your most effective as a therapist. You may feel it is helpful to have an energy protector to ensure that you do not absorb any negativity from your patients.

RIGHT SOME THERAPISTS WEAR CRYSTAL JEWELLERY TO PROTECT THEM IN THEIR WORK.

CRYSTALS AND YOUR PATIENTS

There are many crystal therapy techniques that can be incorporated into other complementary therapies.

Often your patients can find it helpful to hold a crystal during the therapy session. This helps to encourage them to participate in their own healing process. The crystal may act as a point of focus, it can help the patient to stay grounded within their healing process, or it may aid a release of redundant energies. Occasionally you may wish to suggest that your patient takes this crystal home with them in order to carry on some self-healing work on their own. The crystal can act as an on-going support and link between you in between sessions.

Some therapists have a selection of crystals in their therapy room and suggest the patient chooses one to hold during the session. The crystal chosen will often give the therapist helpful and relevant insight.

ABOVE YOUR THERAPIST MAY ASK YOU TO CHOOSE, WITH EYES CLOSED, FROM A BOWL OF POLISHED STONES.

Alternatively, you could have a bowl of polished stones. The patient affirms that they will attract what they need for their healing and then, with their eyes closed, he or she picks a stone from the bowl. It can be most illuminating to note the reaction of the patient and discover whether or not this is a crystal that would have been consciously chosen.

It can also be extremely effective to place crystals around your patient. However, using crystals in this way creates a risk of the patient becoming unearthed (*see* p.79). The trained therapist will be able to recognize this and may decide to also place an earthing crystal by the patient's feet, or perhaps under the chair or couch in line with the base chakra.

Crystals may be placed beneath a chair or massage couch. Although these can be quite unobtrusive, unless your patient is visiting you specifically for crystal therapy, we feel it is ethical to point out that you incorporate crystal energy into your work.

Crystals can also be used to create a safe and sacred space in which you can carry out your usual treatment or therapy. You may be able to work within a three-dimensional energized geometric shape created by placing crystals in certain formations. Popular choices might include a pyramid or six-pointed Star of David. These techniques can be very powerful because they draw upon the ancient power of sacred geometry as well as the energy of the crystals themselves. As with all things powerful, it is advised that caution be exercised when employing this type of technique. Ideally seek professional training.

The trained therapist will be aware of the advantages and possible dangers associated with this specialized form of energy work and will take great care in the dismantling as well as construction of these powerful shapes. It is important to ensure that the patient's aura is not damaged due to prematurely entering or exiting a prepared space.

AROMATHERAPY AND MASSAGE

Crystals can be stored next to or near to your oils to help keep them fresh and vibrant. They may also be attuned to imbue the oils with their own particular crystalline vibration or, if you specifically tune the crystal, to a vibration of your choice.

Some aromatherapists and masseurs like to include a crystal in their bodywork. Clearly it is good practice to use smooth crystals such as the tumble stones or spheres. Although rather more expensive to buy than tumble stones, massage wands that have rounded ends are also very effective and are now far more commercially available.

Sometimes during a treatment it is appropriate to leave the person within the healing process and stop massaging for a while. You may want to place a few crystals on the back or the part of the body you have been working on at this time to help continue the healing process. You can then cover up this part of the body, leaving the crystals to carry on your good work and you can continue massaging another area of the body or let the patient rest for a while.

Some therapists like to use particular crystals with certain oils, for example if using rose oil to release an emotion they may feel it is appropriate to draw upon the qualities of rose quartz as well. This may be considered a good working relationship for working with the heart chakra.

RIGHT ESSENTIAL OILS MAY STAY FRESH LONGER IF STORED NEAR TO A CRYSTAL.

ABOVE SELF-MASSAGE WITH A CRYSTAL IS A QUICK AND EASY TREATMENT TO PERFORM AT THE END OF A LONG, HARD DAY.

SELF-MASSAGE

This is a useful pick-me-up treatment for tired therapists and patients alike.

97

Take a smooth crystal such as a large tumble stone or sphere, and use this to gently massage any areas of the body that feel in need of an extra bit of tender, loving care. You will discover that this is a simple and yet extremely pleasant way of stroking away the stresses of a hard day.

A wonderful way to refresh tired aching feet, after a long day at work, is to immerse your feet in a big bowl of tumble stones. Allow your feet to become covered in all those smooth stones and massage the painful or tender areas that are so difficult to reach. Remember to cleanse the crystals afterwards.

REFLEXOLOGY

The patient can benefit from holding crystals during a reflexology treatment. Some reflexologists like to use a crystal occasionally, rather than their thumbs, to activate various energy points throughout the feet. Usually only the lightest pressure is needed, and sometimes the crystal does not quite touch the skin. The crystal, it seems, works at a different frequency and vibratory level to the physical hand, allowing a greater range of healing vibrations to be offered to the patient.

ACUPUNCTURE AND ACUPRESSURE

Instead of using needles or fingers, crystals can be used to activate the various acupressure points throughout the body. To clear a meridian, some therapists find it very effective to take two quartz points or wands and apply them to two polarizing pressure points working either on the physical body or a few inches off the body. Some patients respond more effectively to crystals, particularly when working off the body, rather than having physical pressure or needles applied to the skin.

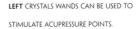

LEFT CRYSTALS WANDS CAN BE USED TO STIMULATE ACUPRESSURE POINTS.

FAVOURITE CRYSTALS

There are more than 3,000 different minerals and crystals known in the world at this time. Many beautifully illustrated books are available that present information about different crystals. The aim of this chapter, therefore, is to introduce you to a few of the more popular and commonly known crystals that you will almost certainly encounter, and may wish to acquire as you begin to explore the crystal realm.

All the crystals described below are easily available and have, in our opinion, many different applications that will make them versatile and hopefully likely choices to become part of your crystal healing starter kit.

For each of these crystals we give a basic gemmological and physical breakdown:-

Family group name: This will tell you the family group name of which a particular crystal is a member. Some of these groups are large with many varieties, some are much smaller. These have only been included where applicable. For example, celestite is not part of a family group, whereas quartz consists of many different varieties.

Hardness: Hardness is measured on the Mohs Scale. Based on the Mohs system, all crystals are given a hardness value rated on a scale between 1 and 10. The hardest known natural substance is diamond therefore it is rated as 10. The next hardest is the corundum family, which is rated at 9. Talc, rated one, is the softest mineral. The softer stones will damage easily.

Chemical composition: The actual chemical components that form the crystal.

Crystal system: Every crystal will fall into one of the seven different crystal systems, unless it is amorphous or a rock. The crystal system gives insight in to how the crystal has 'grown' at a molecular level. It may be considered the basic blueprint or pattern of how the crystal forms by building layer upon layer of atoms and electrons in a very concise arrangement (*see* p.17).

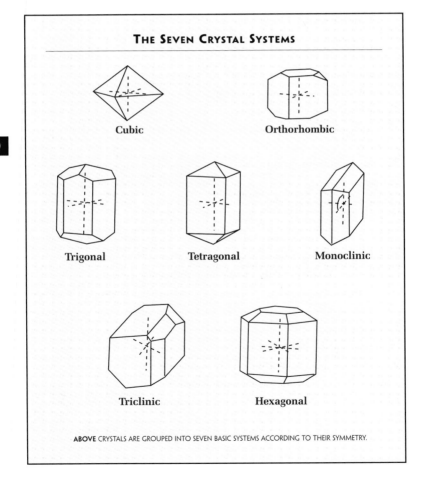

THE SEVEN CRYSTAL SYSTEMS

Cubic

Orthorhombic

Trigonal

Tetragonal

Monoclinic

Triclinic

Hexagonal

ABOVE CRYSTALS ARE GROUPED INTO SEVEN BASIC SYSTEMS ACCORDING TO THEIR SYMMETRY.

Colour(s): The range of various hues and colours in which you might expect to find a particular crystal.

Countries of origin: There are pockets of crystals dotted all around the world, but we have listed only the areas that either produce a lot of crystals or feature an unusual specimen.

Crystal formation: The form in which crystals grow or are usually found. This section will take into account the various formations in which crystals have been discovered to date.

CLEAR QUARTZ (ALSO KNOWN AS ROCK CRYSTAL)

Family group name: Quartz

Hardness: 7

Chemical composition: Silicon and oxygen

Crystal system: Trigonal

Colour(s): Clear to milky opaque

Countries of origin: Outstanding examples found in Brazil, Madagascar, the US

Crystal formation: Single prismatic crystals, group, geodes, crystalline pieces

This is often considered the ultimate healing crystal. The Ancients used to call clear quartz 'frozen water from heaven'. Clear quartz, as its name suggests, is clear, ideally almost as clear as glass, although it can also be milky to such an extent as to appear opaque.

Quartz or silicon dioxide is one of the most commonly found minerals on the Earth, which in its various forms, is thought to cover a large proportion of the Earth's crust. Sandy beaches are in fact largely made up of vast quantities of quartz fragments; sand obtains its golden colour through the staining of water-borne iron.

ABOVE CLEAR QUARTZ HAS BEEN USED AS A HEALING STONE FOR THOUSANDS OF YEARS.

Quartz crystals often have interesting 'inclusions'. These are caused by substances that can be seen within the crystal. For example, other minerals such as tourmaline, rutile, mica and actinolite can sometimes be seen inside quartz crystals.

Quartz crystals occur in six-sided prism shapes with a termination made up of six roughly triangular faces coming to a point. Some crystals may have a termination or point at both ends – this is known as a double-terminated or bi-terminated crystal. Quartz can also be found in clusters – groups of crystal points with one end of each point embedded into the matrix rock. It is also possible to find chunks of quartz without external crystal symmetry.

Generally, quartz crystals command a higher value if they have good, clean, unbroken tips, and a very clear glass-like degree of translucency. A lower market value is often placed on crystals that are chipped or broken and those with milky parts to them.

Quartz is found all over the world. There are quartz deposits scattered throughout England, although, with a few exceptions, none are particularly spectacular. The majority of quartz crystals found in shops and museums are usually imported from countries including Brazil, Madagascar and the US.

We find that clear quartz can be used to direct energy and to strengthen the energy link to the Earth or the Heavens. Clear quartz is believed by many to help focus concentration and bring clarity of thought. Rock crystal spheres are frequently used for divination or crystal ball gazing.

Most people when starting to collect crystals will buy at least one quartz crystal. However, many people report feeling more comfortable with rose quartz or amethyst, which is perceived to have a more gentle or nurturing feel than clear quartz, which some people can find too intense or too powerful. There will be times when this type of energy is exactly what is needed, however. Only you can judge whether you need a clear quartz or not. Even if you are not very attracted to clear quartz, you might find it useful to have as a part of your starter kit. It may help to remember that clear quartz carries white light and therefore all the colours of the spectrum, enabling it, perhaps, to be a universal healing crystal.

There are no limits to the way clear quartz can be used. For example, it may be placed on or off the body, held by the healer or patient or tuned to hold the vibrationary space within a room. Quartz is often used to neutralize the negative energy thought to radiate from computers and other electrical products. Traditionally quartz crystals are considered to be amplifiers of energy. They will strengthen and potentize anything that they come into contact with.

ROSE QUARTZ
Family group name: Quartz
Hardness: 7
Chemical composition: Silicon and oxygen with manganese
Crystal system: Trigonal
Colour(s): Pale to deep pink to lavender pink
Countries of origin: Africa, Brazil, Madagascar, Spain
Crystal formation: Crystalline, single crystals (small, rare), groups (small crystals, rare)

This is a soft pink-coloured stone with varying degrees of translucence. Some pieces are totally transparent, and others are almost opaque.

The colours vary from a whitish-pink to a deep rose pink. Some stones are an unusual lavender pink. These are usually from Madagascar in the Indian Ocean.

Rose quartz is often found as rough-hewn rocks and sold in pieces known as 'chunks'. Rose Quartz is referred to in this chunk form as 'massive'. It consists of many thousands of rose quartz crystals that have grown through and around one another and 'massed' together, taking up all of the available

ABOVE ROSE QUARTZ IS ONE OF THE MOST POPULAR CRYSTALS, AND CAN BE FOUND IN MOST STARTER KITS.

growing space and losing all the definition of the individual crystals as they naturally occurred. Rose quartz was considered to grow only in this 'massive' formation until the mid-1970s, when a seam of rose quartz crystals was discovered in Brazil. This caused experts to reconsider their opinions, particularly as, a short time after, another seam was discovered.

Although rose quartz crystals are now accepted, they are still extremely rare and therefore relatively expensive. They are also usually very small, certainly in comparison to their clear quartz cousins. It is extremely unusual to find any large natural single rose quartz crystals.

Rose quartz is probably one of the most popular and user-friendly crystals available. As such it is considered by many as an essential crystal for any starter kit.

Rose quartz is often attributed with the quality of love, especially unconditional love, and other matters of the heart. It is thought to have very gentle qualities, probably due to its soft colour, making it safe and accessible to all.

104

You may wish to consider acquiring two or three rose quartz pieces when planning your healing starter kit. When looking for a piece of rose quartz, consider the quality of the colour and the degree of the clarity. Rose quartz that displays very pure clear colour, without traces of brown iron staining, and that has a high degree of translucency is considered high quality and is therefore more expensive. However, as you become more sensitive to crystal energies it will be of more importance to tune into the crystal's energy and not just its appearance.

ABOVE LOVE AND ROMANCE ARE COMMONLY ASSOCIATED WITH THE SOFT AND TENDER ROSE QUARTZ.

As with clear quartz, rose quartz can be used in many ways. It can be a calming stone and as such is an ideal crystal for holding and playing a part in meditation practice. Patients can also be given a piece to hold while you give them healing.

It is commonly considered to be a relatively safe crystal to use, although it has also been described as the iron fist within a velvet glove. Amongst other qualities, it has an enduring strength that is often deceptive and goes unnoticed at first.

Large tumble stones can be used to massage the physical body, and may be combined, if you are suitably trained, with reflexology or massage therapy. In fact, virtually all crystal healing techniques can incorporate rose quartz, whether it be chakra healing, working on the subtle bodies or placing patterns on or around the body (providing of course that these techniques are appropriate to that particular patient).

ABOVE ROSE QUARTZ CAN BE USED IN REFLEXOLOGY TREATMENT BY A SUITABLY TRAINED THERAPIST.

As mentioned previously, rose quartz is often said to symbolize love. This is because rose quartz is associated with soothing qualities such as gentleness, forgiveness, comfort, tenderness and softness.

Generally, rose quartz is attributed to opening to the higher consciousness and opening the heart centre, so all love issues and issues related to that will apply.

However, a more recent and less traditional idea is that of helping humans to fall in love with the concept of being on Earth and being of service while on this planet. This makes rose quartz a particularly useful crystal for people who are finding it hard to cope with life within the physical realm.

AMETHYST

Family group name: Quartz
Hardness: 7
Chemical composition: Silicon and oxygen with iron
Crystal system: Trigonal
Colour(s): Pale lilac to deep purple black
Countries of origin: Brazil, Uruguay
Crystal formation: Crystalline, single crystals, groups
or clusters, geodes

Amethyst is another extremely well known crystal. Its beautiful purple colour has been admired for many thousands of years, leading to its use as a popular gemstone.

Amethyst comes in a range of wonderful hues, varying from a very pale lilac to a very deep (almost black) purple colour. Similarly, the degree of clarity ranges from total translucency to total opacity. Banded or chevron amethyst is also widely available. This has white layers between the purple colour, although these examples are more commonly found as tumble stones.

Mineral dealers consider the crystals with pure, deep purple colours with good clarity to be high quality. However, they will also pay a premium for large undamaged crystals with little or no matrix (bed) rock. As you become more sensitive to the crystal energies, you may wish to look at the different degrees of colour to see what is most appropriate for you and your needs.

Amethyst can be found as beds or groups of crystal points. These are often known as 'clusters' or as amethyst 'druse'. Amethyst often forms in what appear to be hollow boulders, which from the outside look quite unexciting, however, when opened, magical caves full of amethyst glisten inside. Sometimes these boulders form natural shapes known as cornucopia (horns of plenty). These are ideal for placing other crystals or your hands inside. Cave-like shapes known as churches or 'Madonnas' are also available. These are basically natural boulders that have been cut open using a diamond saw.

The leading edges are polished smooth and the base prepared in such a way as to allow the piece to stand. Single crystals are sometimes found with one termination but rarely the prismatic length, which is more common in clear quartz crystals. Chunks of amethyst can be found in the same way as with rose quartz. Tumble stones of amethyst are frequently seen.

Amethyst is believed to have uplifting, transformative qualities that can be used for raising vibrations. It is therefore traditionally associated with meditation and changes in consciousness. Amethyst is often associated with the spiritual channel and used in conjunction with higher crown chakra-type activities.

Amethyst has also been connected with the ability to absorb negativity. Drinking tumblers have been carved from amethyst in the belief that they will protect the heavy drinker from a hangover the following day.

Many therapists who do not practise crystal healing nonetheless like to have an amethyst, perhaps in the form of a large display piece, in their therapy room. This acts as a 'spiritual air freshener' to ensure that the vibrations stay clear, clean and balanced and that the spiritual influence is ever-present.

A single amethyst crystal can be placed on or around the body or directed to various points located on the body. It can be ideal when held in the hand as an aid to meditation. Working with this crystal may also increase your sensitivity to subtle energies, enabling a greater awareness of the Divine influence that is constantly surrounding you.

You may also wish to use an amethyst cluster as a bed to 'house' your other crystals, keeping them cleansed and highly energized. However, be aware of placing your crystals carefully. Consider the hardness factors of stones placed on your cluster – harder stones may damage your amethyst if carelessly placed, and the amethyst may also scratch softer stones.

NB: Amethyst may fade if exposed to bright sunlight for prolonged periods of time.

IRON PYRITE (FOOL'S GOLD)

Hardness: 6–6.5
Chemical composition: Iron sulphide
Crystal system: Cubic
Colour(s): Metallic gold
Countries of origin: India, Spain, Uruguay
Crystal formation: Single crystals, groups or clusters

Iron pyrite is usually gold-coloured because of its high iron content. It is a heavy solid mineral and is always opaque.

Iron pyrite forms in several ways that are all variations on the cubic theme. You may find examples of single crystals that have formed within their own growing environment. These are extraordinary looking crystals because they are perfect cubes with faces so smooth it is difficult to believe that they have not been manufactured. Sometimes several pyrite crystals form within the same growing environment. This can result in fascinating shapes such as clusters (a group of crystals all growing together in an almost random way). Occasionally 'stairways' of pyrite can be found. These are naturally forming cubes of pyrite connected in such a way as to resemble a series of steps leading off from one large cube at the bottom, with progressively smaller cubes attached to each other and reaching out.

Iron pyrite may also be found among other rocks and minerals. The most famous example of this is lapiz lazuli, which is dependent on the pyrite for its gold flecks. Clear quartz can also occasionally be seen with a dusting of pyrite crystals covering parts of its surface.

Iron pyrite is found in many parts of the world, including Spain, which is particularly renowned for its unusually high quality specimens of pyrite including the 'stairways'. It can also be found in South America and India.

Traditionally, pyrite is considered to be a 'grounding' stone. It has a heavy, metallic and solid quality, which is thought to help people to keep their feet on the ground. Sometimes pyrite is thought to be a stone of prosperity. Some people like to hold it and hope it will attract money and prosperity into their lives!

From the healer's point of view, pyrite is usually worked with as a single crystal or a cluster of several crystals. These can be placed on or around the patient's body depending on the healer's intention. For example, iron pyrite can be used as an earthing stone.

ABOVE PYRITE IS ASSOCIATED WITH PROSPERITY AND WEALTH, SO IS A FAVOURITE STONE FOR THOSE WISHING TO ATTRACT MONEY.

Pyrite does not particularly like being immersed in water, which may cause it to oxidize and lose something of its attractive appearance. You may prefer therefore to cleanse it by smudging it with incense or smudge mix, using sound, visualization, candlelight or sunlight.

109

MALACHITE
Hardness: 4
Chemical composition: Copper carbonate
Crystal system: Monoclinic
Colour(s): Green-light and dark swirls
Countries of origin: Former Soviet Union, Zaire
Crystal formation: Crystalline chunks, rarely crystal

Malachite is a rich, vibrant, predominantly green-coloured stone. It often has layers, banding, or swirls of colour in which its rich green colour is interspersed with light or dark layers. Copper is the primary cause of its colour.

Malachite crystals are occasionally seen, although you are far more likely to see larger pieces that have been worked in order to display the beautiful ringed effect caused by the 'botryoidal' growing process.

Malachite is a soft stone and is therefore easy to carve into the numerous animal figurines, ashtrays and jewellery that is now available from many gift and craft shops around the world.

Although well known for aesthetic reasons, malachite is less well renowned for its healing qualities. A polished piece of malachite can make a very useful addition to your starter kit. However, in addition to being comfortable to hold in the hand, it could also be taped or bandaged onto the body. It is suitable to be placed on or around the body during a healing act.

Some healer's consider malachite to have a very absorbent quality and say it is particularly useful for drawing off inflammations,

---

CAUTION

SPECIAL SAFETY NOTE: Malachite is very TOXIC in its raw form and when it is being worked. The powder or dust that is displaced during the carving process is highly poisonous and has been found to damage the lungs of craftspeople who work with it. Material that has been polished will normally be stabilized. This will seal the outer surface and stop loose particles from coming away.

Because of its toxic potential, we do not believe that malachite is suitable for making gem essences in water, unless, of course, you have the training and knowledge required for this very specialized form of healing. In addition, malachite should not be licked or placed in the mouth. This could have very serious consequences. Simply working with the raw mineral and inhaling the dust can produce a toxic reaction. If you feel strongly attracted to working with the raw mineral, always ensure that you wash your hands thoroughly afterwards and warn anyone else who touches it to do the same. Keep it out of reach of children or pets.

infections, toxins etc. Others find it useful for balancing issues connected with the heart and solar plexus chakras. Some find it helpful to connect you with the Earth. These balancing and absorbing qualities mean that malachite could be used in many ways for comfort and support by the healer or the patient.

CELESTITE (ALSO KNOWN AS CELESTINE)
Family group name: Celestite or celestine
Hardness: 3–3.5
Chemical composition: Strontium sulphate
Crystal system: Orthorhombic
Colour(s): Pale Blue, colourless to greenish blue
Countries of origin: Madagascar, UK, the US
Crystal formation: Single crystals, clusters and geodes

Most of the celestite generally available occurs in a beautiful pale blue-grey colour, which is largely imported from Madagascar. There are also whitish-colourless varieties that have been discovered in other locations such as the US and deposits are also known to exist in south-west England. However, it is usually the clear pale blue-grey crystals that are highly prized by healers.

Celestite is most usually found as single crystals growing within a group or geode. Because celestite is a member of the orthorhombic crystal system it forms as four sided, sometimes square crystals, with a short, almost dome-shaped top or termination. You may find a piece of celestite that has been shaped into an egg or sphere, with one side left open allowing you to see inside a cave of celestite crystals. These make particularly attractive features as well as useful healing tools.

RIGHT CELESTITE IS A SOFT STONE, MAKING IT PARTICULARLY SUSCEPTIBLE TO DAMAGE.

Celestite is rarely seen as tumble stones or jewellery, as it is a particularly soft stone, and it is difficult to achieve a high standard of surface polish. It is easy to damage celestite, particularly if the crystal is likely to come into contact with harder materials such as other tumbled minerals or jewellery. Celestite is also vulnerable to dust, which contains other minerals often harder than 3.5 and is therefore likely to scratch the surface if carelessly wiped clean. Be aware of placing celestite close to harder materials such as amethyst, clear quartz, rose quartz etc. as it will very quickly become damaged if physical contact is made.

Some pieces of celestite also seem to fade if they are left a long time in the sunlight – so caution should be exercised in the positioning of your celestite crystals.

Traditionally, celestite is considered one of the stones associated with movement and the dismantling of barriers. Use celestite to help you clarify the direction to take when faced with a multitude of confusing options.

Celestite can help to raise the consciousness during meditation and allow you to experience a spiritual realm that may have eluded you before.

We feel that celestite might be a suitable crystal to include in your starter kit. You might use it in the meditation room or in the space where you regularly pray and contemplate as a stone for inspiration and spiritual guidance. This crystal can help to spotlight particular problems associated with spiritual development and will guide you through in a direct, almost brutal, way.

You may find that fundamental life changes will occur at the same time that you bring celestite into your life. Only work with celestite when and if you feel personally attracted to its vibration and spectacular beauty.

Some people find the energy of this crystal extremely potent and occasionally disturbing, particularly if they are attached to issues that ideally should be released. Use it with caution as a personal crystal only!

TOURMALINE

Family group name: Tourmaline
Hardness: 7–7.5
Chemical composition: Varies depending on the colour and variety but usually includes iron, magnesium, lithium, manganese
Crystal system: Trigonal
Colour(s): All colours including mixtures, black and colourless
Countries of origin: Brazil, Madagascar
Crystal formation: Single crystals, clusters and geodes

Tourmaline crystals often occur as long, thin, almost needle-like crystals. It belongs to the same crystal system as quartz. However, rather than having six sides in a prismatic hexagonal form, tourmaline crystals tend to have three, larger rounded sides interspersed with three much smaller sides, deep grooves or striations running vertically the length of the crystal. The termination will be almost like a pyramid, with three triangular faces coming to a point.

113

Tourmaline occurs in all colours, depending on the minerals that were present while it formed. Tourmaline not only occurs as single crystals but also as groups or clusters of crystals. It can be obtained as reasonably inexpensive tumbled pieces or rough chunks. It can also be encountered as rather more expensive single crystals or groups of crystals that are the same or multi-coloured. For the crystal connoisseur, tourmaline also lends itself exceptionally well to fine jewellery. However, these items are usually expensive. Tourmaline is also often found as an 'inclusion' in other crystals. This is especially obvious in transparent crystals such as quartz, which are then categorized as 'tourmilated quartz'.

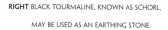

RIGHT BLACK TOURMALINE, KNOWN AS SCHORL,
MAY BE USED AS AN EARTHING STONE.

Different coloured tourmaline crystals are known by different names. Rubelite is the pinkish-red variety, indicolite is blue to blue-green and schorl is the black variety. However, it is acceptable to simply refer to 'pink tourmaline', 'green tourmaline' etc. Tourmaline crystals often display varying shades or even different colours depending on how you view them. It is interesting to view the tourmaline through the side and then lengthways. A crystal that may seem densely black from one angle may in fact turn out to be a beautiful deep green colour from another. This is caused by a phenomenon known as 'pleochroism', which occurs in many coloured crystals due to the way light behaves within the crystal structure.

The different colours that tourmaline comes in makes it very attractive to collectors as well as healers. Some tourmaline features 'colour zoning', which means that a single crystal of tourmaline could have different bands of colour. A single crystal might change from green to pink to red throughout its length clearly, showing three distinct colour zones. This 'colour zoning' also occurs from the outside working into the crystal. Often you will see 'slices' of tourmaline that show very beautiful patterns. One of the most well-known forms is watermelon tourmaline, which, like its namesake, is green on the outside and pinky-red on the inside. Very intricate patterns can occur with these slices, including fantastic triangulations. There are even some patterns that seem to resemble a figure with arms extended like a figure on a cross. One German geologist has looked at the sacredness and geometry of the patterns formed by tourmaline and concluded that these extraordinary crucifix-like patterns make it a most mystical stone.

Tourmaline is very varied in its shape, form and colour and its healing applications are equally varied. Small pieces of tourmaline may be placed on or around the body, on chakra points, meridian lines, etc. The healer may wish to hold a wand, or a single crystal of tourmaline, and direct energy through different parts of the body. The patient may be encouraged to hold pieces of tourmaline. The solid, thicker black tourmaline chunks and large crystals suit some patients and healers as earthing stones. They can be placed under the patient's chair or be held by the patient to keep them well grounded. The possibilities are almost as limitless as the different forms of tourmaline crystals. Because of this versatility, tourmaline in some form is a valuable asset to include within a healing kit.

CITRINE

Family group name : Quartz
Hardness: 7
Chemical composition: Silicon and oxygen with iron
Crystal system: Trigonal
Colour(s): Light yellow through gold to brown
Countries of origin: Brazil and Uruguay
Crystal formation: Crystalline, single crystals, groups and geodes

Citrine is reasonably rare in its natural form because a number of factors are needed for it to evolve.

115

Citrine starts out as a fully formed amethyst. Once the amethyst crystal has formed, and laid dormant in the Earth for a while, it may again be subjected to heat, perhaps due to thermal activity within the crust of the Earth. At approximately 450°C, the amethyst will change colour to become citrine or alternatively it may change colour in localized places to become ametrine, which is a mix of purple and yellow amethyst and citrine. If heated to above 450°C, the amethyst will lose all colour and become opaque white.

ABOVE NATURAL CITRINE IS COMPARATIVELY RARE, THOUGH COMMERCIALLY HEATED FORMS ARE WIDELY AVAILABLE.

Much of the citrine that is commercially available is in fact artificially heated amethyst.

Purists would argue that it is not 'real' citrine because it has not been naturally heated in the Earth. Generally, 'natural' citrine is much more expensive and relatively scarce. It is also often quite a pale colour. However, it is very difficult for the untrained person, who is unlikely to have access to gem-testing equipment, to distinguish between natural and manipulated citrine. As a general guideline, we would recommend that you follow your intuition and work with the feel of the stone. Monitor your reactions. If you feel comfortable and happy with the citrine crystal, then it is quite in order to continue to use it.

Citrine is renowned for its beautiful golden-yellow colour. The colour can vary greatly and citrine can be found ranging from a deep orange-brown colour that can appear very dense and opaque, to totally translucent lemon-yellow.

Citrine normally forms as single crystals or groups of crystals and occasionally as geodes. Large chunks of 'massive' material have also been discovered. If these are high-quality natural material they will often be carved into statues and other crystal works of art. Rough chunks and tumbled pieces of citrine are commonly available, along with worked pieces carved into massage wands, spheres, pyramids etc.

Citrine is traditionally associated with words such as inspiration and abundance. Some people find it a useful stone for attracting money and associate it with gold and riches. Other people associate it with cosmic gold and feel it is a stone that inspires wisdom and enlightenment. It can be viewed as a representation of the golden light of the heavens.

Most people find this a happy, uplifting and energizing stone. Some feel it reminds them of the pleasures of summer giving them a chance to get outside and reunite with nature if only via meditation. It can be held by healer or patient or placed on or around the body by the healer.

Some say the deeper orange-coloured crystals should be used on the lower energy centres.

LAPIS LAZULI

Hardness: 5.5

Chemical composition: Contains various minerals including pyrite, alcite, lazurite, noseite hauyanite silicate

Crystal system: N/A – all the minerals that make up this rock except calcite are part of the cubic crystal system

Colour(s): Blue with white plus gold flecks

Countries of origin: Afghanistan, Chile, China, Former Soviet Union

Lapis lazuli is, strictly speaking, not a crystal but a rock made up of different crystalline materials, all of which are cubic except for calcite (which is trigonal). This is why in some texts you may see lapis listed as a cubic crystal.

The gold traces that can be seen in lapis, for which it is so famous, are, in fact, pyrite and not gold as is commonly thought. Undoubtedly the most distinguishing feature of lapis is its fabulous luxuriant blue colour with gold traces.

More expensive material has no obvious white in it (which comes from the inclusion of calcite) and a deep rich blue colour with obvious 'gold' flecks.

Lazurite crystals (which are often called lapis crystals and indeed are one of the six crystals found in lapis) are very rarely found. Lapis is more usually found in chunks and boulders, which are often polished and shaped.

Lapis is enhanced and its colourful properties shown to the full extent of their beauty when polished, so this is the usual way it will be displayed in the mineral dealer's stock.

Healers, however, may prefer natural chunks, which are now becoming more readily available as the demand for the natural material becomes greater.

ABOVE LAPIS LAZULI IS FAMED FOR ITS RICH BLUE COLOUR STREAKED WITH GOLD.

Lapis has been known for thousands of years. It figures strongly in our ancient traditions and history.

Its name derives from a number of languages and their derivatives. It originally took its name from *lazward* an Arabic word for blue. It was then known as *lazurius* from the Latin, *lazure* (French), which in turn came from *azul* (Arabic) and *lazur* (Persian). Each of these means a 'very special blue'.

It was considered by ancient manuscripts to be the sapphire of the Ancient Greeks. Its healing powers are even mentioned in the *Ebers Papyrus* (dating around 1600 BC), where it is mentioned as a cure for cataracts.

If an unpolished piece of lapis is regularly handled, you will find that the oils that exude naturally from the skin are absorbed and these will start to polish and brighten the piece. Some people like to use various essential oils and combine the properties of lapis with these essential oils, which they imbue into their piece of lapis so you have a wonderful healing piece that you have personalized over a period of time.

Lapis is often associated with ancient Egypt perhaps because it features strongly in Egyptian mythology, as well as being used to decorate ancient jewellery as well and burial masks.

Some people feel that it is a very useful stone for working with past life experiences and helping to unlock or clear issues that predate the present. Another aspect of lapis is its ability to offer protection, particularly when working in a spiritual capacity and exercising the brow chakra.

Lapis is also thought to have a regal quality that can offer a powerful energy to those perhaps looking for a little more self-esteem. You might consider using lapis to assist you in healing and meditation techniques if you feel you require these sort of properties.

Lapis is a stone that may be too powerful for some patients and should be used with caution. Some would say it is more appropriate to use it for personal development.

TURQUOISE

Hardness: 5–6

Chemical composition: Phosphate

Crystal system: Triclinic

Colour(s): Greenish-yellow light blue

Countries of origin: China, Egypt, Former Soviet Union, Iran, the US

Crystal formation: Cryptocrystalline, massive, nodules.

Turquoise is often opaque to bright blue or greenish blue. Until 1911, when turquoise crystals were found in Virginia, USA, turquoise was not believed to be crystalline. It is normally found as massive or nodular aggregates and boulders are found in Iran, Tibet, France, Chile and the US.

The word turquoise comes from the French, meaning 'Turkish stone'. Historically, turquoise was thought to originate in Turkey, but it is often mined in Iran, and travels to Europe via Turkey.

The Navajo were known to carry a personal piece of turquoise. If thrown into a river, it was believed to bring rain. Pieces have been found set in door lintels to keep evil spirits away.

Turquoise has always been widely simulated because of its precious status. Plastics and ceramics are often sold masquerading as turquoise. Howlite, a naturally white stone containing veins similar to those in turquoise, is dyed light blue and passed off as turquoise. Today many 'natural' pieces of turquoise are 'colour-stabilized', impregnated with wax, plastic, sodium silicate or dye to enhance the colour. Turquoise can also be reconstituted. This involves grinding up very small pieces to produce a powder that is then set solid with a form of epoxy resin. The finished product can be easily carved into new shapes ready for mounting into jewellery.

ABOVE TURQUOISE IS A VERY POPULAR STONE FOR FASHIONING INTO PIECES OF JEWELLERY.

There are many traditions attached to turquoise. For example, it was thought to change colour to warn its wearer of imminent danger. It has been suggested that a modern-day use of turquoise might be to protect against environmental pollutants. Turquoise is claimed to have a calming and peaceful quality, improving meditation and promoting peace of mind. Turquoise has often been associated with success, happiness and the bringing of friendships and love into the life of the wearer. There is also a theory that turquoise can aid

anorexia nervosa. It is believed to increase the circulatory flow to muscular tissues, particularly if worn on fingers as rings.

LEFT IT IS THOUGHT THAT TURQUOISE MAY AFFORD SOME PROTECTION AGAINST ENVIRONMENTAL POLLUTION.

FURTHER READING

Baer, Randall and Vicki, *Windows of Light*, Harper & Row

Bonewitz, Ra, *The Cosmic Crystal Spiral*, Element

Brennan, Barbara Ann, *Hands of Light*, Bantam

Burgess, Jacquie, *Healing with Crystals*, Gill & Macmillan

Burgess, Jacquie, *Crystals for Life*, Gill & Macmillan

Cassandra, Gurudas, *Gem Elixirs and Vibrational Healing*,

Hackl, Monnica, *Crystal Energy*, Element, 1994

Hall, Cally, *Gem Stones*, Dorling Kindersley

Harrison, Stephanie and Kleiner, Barbara, *The Crystal Wisdom Kit*, Connections, 1999

Harrison, Stephanie and Kleiner, Barbara, *Crystal Wisdom for Love*, Simon & Schuster, 1999

Harrison, Stephanie and Kleiner, Barbara, *Crystal Wisdom for Personal Growth*, Simon & Schuster, 1999

Harrison, Stephanie and Kleiner, Barbara, *Crystal Wisdom for Personal Health*, Simon & Schuster, 1999

Harrison, Stephanie and Kleiner, Barbara, *Crystal Wisdom for Prosperity*, Simon & Schuster, 1999

Holbeche, Soozi, *The Power of Gems and Crystals*, Piaktus

Gardner, Gordon, *Colour and Crystals*, The Crossing Press

Gienger, Michael, *Crystal Power, Crystal Healing*, Blandford

Kozminsky, Isodore, *The Magic and Science of Jewels and Stones*

Kunz, George Frederick, *The Curious Lore of Precious Stones*, Dover

Lilly, Sue and Simon, *Crystal Doorways*, Capall Bann

Meadows, Kenneth, *Shamanic Experience*, Element, 1991

Meadows, Kenneth, *The Medicine Way*, Element, 1990

Mercer, Ian, *Crystals*, HMSO

Oldfield, Harry and Coghill, Roger, *The Dark Side of the Brain*, Element, 1988

Shapiro, Debbie, *The Bodymind Workbook*, Element

Simpson, Liz, *The Book of Crystal Healing*, Gaia

Symes, R and Harding, R, *Crystal and Gem*, Dorling Kindersley

Williams, Tom, *The Complete Illustrated Guide to Chinese Medicine*, Element, 1996

The International College
of Crystal Healing
46 Lower Green Road
Esher
Surrey KT10 8HD
Tel: 0208 398 7252
Fax: 0208 398 4237

ICCH offers a formal practitioner training programme for those who wish to become professional crystal therapists. The course takes place part-time over a minimum period of two years. The comprehensive syllabus incorporates the use of many different crystal healing techniques and students have access to a wide range of crystals.

The Affiliation of Crystal
Healing Organizations (ACHO)
PO Box 344
Manchester M60 2EZ
Tel/Fax: 01479 841450

(To receive a copy of the ACHO Practitioner Register, please send a SAE to the above address.)

The Academy of Crystal and
Natural Healing (ACNH) –
Member of ACHO
Craig Gowan
Carrbridge
Invernesshire PH23 3AX
Principal: Sue Richter
Tel: 01479 841257

Academy of Crystal
Enlightenment (ACE) – Member
of ACHO
9 Courthope Road
Greenford
Middlesex UB6 8PZ
Principal: Ivy Smith
Tel: 0181 578 0960

Cornwall School of Crystal
Healing (CSCH) – Member of
ACHO
Morden Farm
Callington
Cornwall PL17 8BY.
Principal: Sue Phillips

Geometrics of Self Healing
(GSH) – Member of ACHO
19 Gorse Green
Bluebell Estate
Peterborough
Cambs PE1 3XB
Principals: Robina Corby and
Maureen Callacher
Tel: 01733 347190/234385

Institute of Advanced Crystal
Healers
(IACH) – Member of ACHO
Turnpike Cottage
Chawleigh
Chumleigh
Devon EX18 7EU
Principals: Diana and Colin
Kingshott

Institute of Crystal and Gem
Therapists (ICGT) – Member of
ACHO
PO Box 6
Exminster
Exeter
Devon EX6 8AY
Principals: Sue and Simon Lilly
Tel: 01392 832005

International Association of
Crystal Healing Therapists
(IACHT) – Member of ACHO
50 Birchfield Drive
Boothtown
Worsley
Manchester
M28 4ND
Principal: Hazel Raven
Tel: 0161 702 8191

The International College of
Crystal Healing (ICCH) –
Member of ACHO
46 Lower Green Road
Esher
Surrey KT10 8HD
Principal: Stephanie Harrison
Tel: 0208 398 7252
Fax: 0208 398 4237

School of White Crystal Healing
(SWCH) – Member of ACHO
Paradise Valley
Glyn Car
Llangynin
St Clears
Carmarthen SA33 4JY
Tel: 01994 230028/230212
Principals: Cathy Roberts and
Nita Ellul
Tel: 01460 52346

Spiritual Venturers Association
(SVA) – Member of ACHO
72 Pasture Road
Goole
East Yorkshire DN14 6HE
Principal: Kathleen
Huddlestone
Tel: 01405 769119

Harry Oldfield
The School of Electro-Crystal
Therapy
117 Long Drive
South Ruislip
Middlesex HA4 0HL
Tel: 0181 841 1716

Jacquie Burgess
Slaney House
Tullow
County Carlow
Ireland
Tel: 00-353 (0)503 51057

Marion Webb de Sisto
38 Armoury Road
London SE8 4LA
Tel: 0181 469 0424

Chloe Asprey
The Cottage
Orestan Lane
Effingham
Surrey KT24 5SN
Tel: 01372 453143

INDEX

127

CRYSTAL
STARTER KIT

Stephanie and Tim Harrison are offering a crystal starter kit
consisting of pieces of the following seven crystals:

Clear quartz

•

Rose quartz

•

Amethyst

•

Citrine

•

Iron pyrites

•

Celestite

•

Malachite

Please note: This offer is only available in the UK mainland due to postage costs.

TO ORDER PLEASE WRITE TO:

ICCH DEPT NPCT, "CRYSTAL STARTER KIT OFFER", 46 LOWER GREEN ROAD, ESHER, SURREY KT10 8HD

CHEQUES TO BE MADE PAYABLE TO "ICCH" PLEASE.

COST £14.95 INCLUDING POSTAGE AND PACKING.